PETER
Apostle of Contrasts

JAMES T. DYET

ACCENT BOOKS
Denver, Colorado

ACCENT BOOKS

A division of Accent Publications, Inc.
12100 W. Sixth Avenue
P.O. Box 15337
Denver, Colorado 80215

Library of Congress Catalog Card Number 81-70776

ISBN 0-89636-077-6

Second Printing

Contents

1
The Disciple
From Fishtown

Standing with a group of tourists in Colonial Williamsburg, Virginia, I looked down at the glob of wet clay on the potter's wheel. There was certainly nothing attractive or valuable about that reddish brown mass of common muck. Then the potter put his hands on it. Deftly, he worked it into shape as the wheel spun around. Soon it emerged as an attractive vase, which anyone would be proud to own. Exposed to the admiring gaze of all who had witnessed its metamorphosis, it offered a silent testimonial to the creative artistry of the potter.

A close observation of the life of the Apostle Peter shows the creative artistry of another potter, the divine Potter. Before God put His hands on Peter and shaped him into a polished, useful vessel, he was a rather rough blob of humanity. And it is precisely this remarkable transformation that draws us to Peter. We see so much of ourselves in his humanness, and we are encouraged to believe that the divine Potter can shape us, too, into vessels reflecting His glory.

Who knows? Maybe Peter was one of those Paul had in mind when he wrote in I Corinthians 1:26-29:

> For ye see your calling, brethren, how that not many wise men after the flesh, not many mighty, not many noble, are called: But God hath chosen the foolish things of the world to confound the wise; and God hath chosen the weak things of the world to confound the things which are mighty; And the base things of the world, and things which are despised, hath God chosen, yea, and things which are not, to bring to nought things that are: That no flesh should glory in his presence.

If God had given an angel the assignment to find a man who could become a leading apostle for the church, where do you suppose he would have looked for such a man? Perhaps he would have taken the fastest air route to Jerusalem and surveyed the ranks of the nobility and the priesthood in hopes of discovering a truly talented, intelligent, well-bred, and proven leader. But his flight and search would have been futile, because

God's man lived in a smelly fish town, far from Jerusalem, and he was neither nobleman nor priest. Rather, he was a rugged fisherman by the name of Simon, and he was destined to become Peter, an apostle of the Lord Jesus Christ and a fisher of men.

John 1:44 identifies Bethsaida as Peter's hometown, whereas other references in the Gospels indicate that he lived in Capernaum (for example, compare Mark 1:21 and 29). Some Bible teachers suggest that Peter must have grown up in Bethsaida and moved to Capernaum when he married. Others believe Bethsaida and Capernaum were almost one and the same, with Bethsaida serving as the fishing sector of the larger community. There is little support for identifying Peter's hometown with Bethsaida Julias, a small city on the east side of the River Jordan in Gaulanitis.

Bethsaida, meaning *house of fish,* and Capernaum soaked up the sun's rays on the northwestern shore of the Sea of Galilee, about two-and-a-half miles southwest of the point where the Jordan flows into the Sea of Galilee. Both were bustling towns in Jesus' lifetime. Bethsaida was a virtual paradise for fishermen because fish in great numbers basked in its warm, springs-fed bay. Capernaum was an especially important city. Situated on the trade route from Damascus to Egypt and the Mediterranean coast, it housed a military garrison of Roman soldiers and a toll station for gathering tax revenue from passing caravans.

Undoubtedly Peter had seen a lot of exciting things in the twin cities—huge catches of fish in the bay, the flashing of Roman swords against the brilliant rays of the sun, caravan drivers handing over piles of clinking coins to customs officers, and merchants haggling with their customers in the marketplace over the prices of imported wares and fashions. But the most exciting thing of all transpired one day when his brother Andrew rushed up to him and blurted out, "We have found the Messiah" (John 1:41).

Andrew apparently had more of a religious bent to his nature than Peter had, for he was one of John the Baptist's disciples until that excitement-packed day when John introduced him to Jesus Christ. Subsequently, Andrew could not rest until he had found Peter and told him the ecstatic news that the Messiah had come to "fish town."

Faith in Jesus Christ works best when it sets off a chain reaction. John the Baptist prepared the way for Andrew to believe in Him. Then Andrew created an itch in Peter's heart for a meeting with Christ. In turn Peter believed and became a pivotal instrument in God's hands to turn thousands to faith in Christ.

What was it that launched such enthusiastic witnessing in the lives of John the Baptist, Andrew, and eventually Peter? Wasn't it a holy enthusiasm for Christ Himself? These men couldn't have been more excited if they had become heirs to a financial fortune than they were over finding Christ.

It has been said that the great evangelist Gypsy Smith displayed this same infectious enthusiasm. He always preached with great compassion and energy. Even at the close of his ministry he displayed as much enthusiasm for preaching the gospel as he did in his earlier days. When someone asked him the secret of his success in reaching so many for Christ over the long stretch of his career, Mr. Smith replied, "I have never lost the wonder of it all."

Enthusiasm's closest cousin is urgency. John the Baptist's witness to Christ was marked by urgency. He was, as Matthew 3:3 points out, "the voice of one crying in the wilderness, Prepare ye the way of the Lord, make his paths straight." Andrew, too, shared this urgency to be the Messiah's spokesman. He just *had* to find Peter and give him the opportunity of a lifetime, the opportunity to meet Jesus Christ.

In his book, *Discipleship Evangelism,* Ken Stephens stresses the vital contribution a sense of urgency gives to evangelism. He suggests:

Urgency is the fuel of evangelism. It's an attitude of mind and heart which senses a need for action which is insistent until the need is satisfied. A church whose people create a warm atmosphere for evangelism is one with an overwhelming sense of urgency. Individuals who are in incessant activity

9

for the lost are doing so because of an urgency which springs from their theology and relationship to Christ. (From *Discipleship Evangelism*, Scottsdale, Arizona, Good Life Productions, 1978, p. 13.)

Isn't it interesting that most Christians think of Peter as impetuous, always blurting out some blusterous comment without thinking? He is presented to us by speakers and writers as a chronic sufferer of foot-in-mouth disease. And certainly there are more than a few proof texts in Scripture to support this view. Before Pentecost Peter often had his tongue in high gear while his mind seemed to be on a slow idle—or stalled! But how different Peter must have been when he first met Jesus Christ. If he opened his mouth during that momentous occasion, it must have been an expression of astonishment. At least there is no mention in Scripture of his saying anything at that time. It may be that Peter was so awestruck by the powerful, penetrating gaze of God's Son that for once in his life he was speechless.

John 1:42 captures in just a few words the high drama of that first meeting of Jesus and the Galilean fisherman. "And when Jesus beheld him, he said, Thou art Simon the son of Jona: thou shalt be called Cephas, which is by interpretation, a stone." These historic words are full of significance.

I remember fondly the good sense of humor Dr. Kenneth Wuest showed in commenting on John 1:42. Although he was an eminent Greek professor at Moody Bible Institute and a well-published author of Greek word studies, Dr. Wuest seemed to enjoy giving his Greek Exegesis students a laugh now and then, and his students always welcomed the break from the burdensome task of wrestling with verb tenses and noun declensions. Although he made his comment in my 1957 Spring Semester class, I can still picture the mischievous twinkle in his Swedish eyes as he said, "Men, the Apostle Peter was a Swede. In John 1:42 Jesus called him Simon, the son of Jona, then he changed the name Simon to Peter. Since Jona means John, Peter was the son of John; that is, he was Peter Johnson. Now, everyone knows that anyone with the name Peter Johnson just has to be a Swede."

Obviously, the significance of John 1:42 lies beyond Dr. Wuest's tongue-in-cheek logic. The fact is, Jesus' pronouncement that Simon's name would become Peter (the Greek form of Cephas, meaning "a rock") shows that He had big plans for this Galilean fisherman. In due time He would mold Peter into a rock, a dependable, unflinching, and solid foundation on which He would build a lasting ministry. So, when He beheld Peter, He looked beyond the rough-hewn fisherman and viewed him as a masterpiece of God's handiwork. In our parenting, discipling, and all other closely knit relationships, let's try to look at individuals as Jesus sees them.

I find it helpful to recognize that God never

makes a mistake in my life or in the life of any Christian. There are no seconds or discards as far as His workmanship is concerned. When He saved us, He fully intended to make us spiritually productive in this life and perfect, eventually. Ephesians 2:10 assures us that "we are his workmanship, created in Christ Jesus unto good works, which God hath before ordained that we should walk in them." Furthermore, Romans 8:29 presents God's unconditional guarantee that He has predestinated each of us to be "conformed to the image of his Son." Knowing all this, the Apostle Paul could tell the Philippian believers that he was "confident of this very thing, that he which hath begun a good work in you will perform it until the day of Jesus Christ" (Philippians 1:6).

Someday Jesus will return for His church. He will descend from Heaven, enter earth's atmosphere, and summon us Christians away from the earth to meet Him in the air (I Thessalonians 4:16,17). Simultaneously He will resurrect the bodies of dead Christians, and together dead and living Christians will receive perfect bodies and a perfect spiritual likeness to Jesus Christ. The Apostle John prophesied this in I John 3:2: "Beloved, now are we the sons of God, and it doth not yet appear what we shall be: but we know that, when he shall appear, we shall be like him; for we shall see him as he is."

Obviously, like Peter, none of us is perfect yet. We all have a long way to go, but quietly and surely God is working in our lives "both to will and to do of his good pleasure" (Philippians 2:13). As someone has observed, "We're not as good as we ought to be, and not as good as we're going to be; but praise God, we're not as bad as we used to be."

I wish you could meet Shelley, a 17-year-old high school girl who became a Christian when she was 16. Her pastor recalls the Sunday she accepted Christ at the conclusion of a morning service. She told him of her search for forgiveness through various religions, knowing that she had had an illegitimate baby, had been hooked on drugs and alcohol, and had been constantly fighting with her mother and step-father. "I want Christ to save me and make my life different," she said. Today, Shelley provides living proof that Christ changes people for the better. She has led her younger sister to the Lord. She works in children's church, is active in her youth group, and never misses an opportunity to participate in testimony time by declaring how great and good the Lord is. Young and old alike are drawn to Shelley. They like being around her because she radiates Christian joy and love.

Of course, not all Christians are consistently pleasant. Occasionally, some of the Lord's people seem to wear horns instead of halos. That's when others prefer not to be around them. For instance, Johnny told his mother one Sunday morning, "I'm not going to Sunday School and church today for two reasons. First, nobody there likes me; and secondly, I don't like any of them."

"You have to go," Johnny's mother replied, "and I'll give you two good reasons. First, you're forty-three years old; and secondly, you're the pastor."

Well, as Peter continued to follow the Lord, he wasn't always pleasant to be around. At times he said the wrong things and did the wrong things, but the Lord patiently and persistently prayed for him and taught him. He never wrote him off as a lost cause, but always saw him as the finished product of divine grace. So, let's follow our Lord's example by praying for one another and helping one another, believing that God's quality workmanship will prevail.

2
Gone Fishin'

It must have been a beautiful morning, that first morning of Peter's brand-new life. Likely, it seemed to Peter that the sunrise had never been so dazzling. As he looked east, likely he saw a brilliance in nature that he had never seen before. The sweeping rays of the sun were flooding rocks and wildflowers, giving the countryside the appearance of an ocean of glittering diamonds and rubies. Even the air seemed especially tangy. All in all, it was sure to be a day that would explode with adventure.

Peter didn't have to wait long for the adventure to begin, because Jesus soon announced to His followers that He was planning an itinerary in Galilee. It was an adventure Peter couldn't resist, so he teamed up with Andrew, James, and John in following Jesus toward Cana.

The group hadn't gone far when Jesus found Philip and challenged him to become a disciple (John 1:43). In turn, Philip located Nathanael and invited him to meet Jesus and see for himself that Jesus was the Messiah (verses 45,46).

In the brief meeting between Jesus and Nathanael, Nathanael confessed faith in Jesus and joined the disciples' band.

It seems that these six disciples accompanied Jesus at various intervals over the next year and a half, but after each mission they returned to their regular occupations. This explains why we find Peter, in Luke 5, busily engaged at cleaning fishing nets, along with his brother Andrew and their business partners, James and John. But the temporary discipleship was about to end, for Jesus was ready to call Peter and his partners into full-time ministry.

Catch the drama. Crowds of eager listeners were pushing and shoving their way closer and closer to Jesus in order to hear every word He was saying. They knew that He spoke the truth—and did so in an easy-to-understand, close-to-the-heart kind of way. So they didn't want to miss a word. They were tired of the pompous, pious, stuffed-shirt rhetoric of the scribes and Pharisees and eager to drink in Jesus' teachings. But in their eagerness, that mass of humanity almost backed Jesus right into the sea.

That's when Jesus saw the four fishermen

cleaning their nets and also saw their two boats bobbing up and down in the shallow water at the shoreline. Immediately He stepped into Peter's boat and asked Peter to pilot it a short distance into the sea—just far enough to keep the people from getting to Him, yet close enough for them to be able to hear what He would say to them. After reaching just the right spot, Jesus sat down in the boat and taught the people (Luke 5:3).

Later on, Jesus gave a command to Peter. "Launch out into the deep, and let down your nets for a draught" (verse 4). This wasn't exactly what Peter wanted to hear. Likely, he had been hoping to hear Jesus say, "It's been a hard day, Peter. Why don't you go on home now, kick off your sandals, eat a good meal, and relax?"

"Master," Peter offered, "we have toiled all night, and have taken nothing: nevertheless at thy word I will let down the net" (verse 5).

Can you sympathize with Peter? He must have been worn out and terribly discouraged when Jesus first appeared on the shore. He had spent an exhausting night, throwing a heavy net into the sea, dragging it back up to the surface, and finding not even one fish in it—and repeating the process over and over again. Finally, he had washed his net, and was ready to head for home. Now Jesus, *a carpenter*, was telling him to throw in the net again.

Have you been feeling like Peter? Perhaps you have gone visiting for your church, week after week after week, without bringing in a single "fish." You're worn out, on the verge of hanging it up. You have a good mind to tell the pastor to find somebody else for visitation! But somehow it seems the Lord doesn't understand how futile your efforts have been or how discouraged you are, because you get the feeling that He is saying, "Try again."

Well, Peter tried again. In obedience to the Lord's command, he and Andrew flung their net into the deep choppy water. And to their astonishment, that umbrella-shaped net filled up with fish. Their excitement must have run high as they watched the net sag, strain, and stretch under the weight of hundreds of fat, flip-floppy fish. Then, when they heard it start snapping, they sent out an SOS to their partners. It was going to take their partners' boat and theirs to haul the fish to shore. Peter had been obedient to the Lord, and the Lord honored that obedience by giving Peter the catch of a lifetime.

Being involved in this miraculous catch of fish was an excellent learning experience for Peter. For one thing, he learned how different things turn out when Christ takes control of a situation and is obeyed. The long night of fishing had been a frustrating episode, but frustration vanished and success arrived just as soon as Jesus took charge of the fishing operation.

Think again about Peter's first words to the Lord before launching out into the deep. "Master, we have toiled all the night, and have taken nothing." Isn't it true that whatever *we* do without the Lord's direction ends with *nothing*? Jesus said in John 15:5, "Without me ye can do nothing." Our Lord doesn't want us to go it alone, depending upon our skills, our talents, our strength, our personality, and our intelligence to produce the results we long to see in our child rearing, in our evangelistic outreach, in our personal growth, and in our ministry to other Christians. He has a better plan for us to follow: trust Him, and obey Him. If we feel frustrated in *our* work for the Lord, rather than driving ourselves to a breakdown, let's be driven to a kneel-down. In prayer, let's turn the controls over to the Lord and trust Him with the results.

Once again, think about Peter's words when the Lord told him to fish in the deep water. "Nevertheless at thy word I will let down the net," he said. How's that for obedient faith? He didn't say, "Show me a sign, Lord. A few good-sized fish leaping out of the deep water would be such an encouraging sign. After all, it has been a long night, and I don't want to row into the deep water unless you give me some evidence that the fishing there is going to be good." Clearly, Peter chose to obey the word of the Lord instead of giving in to the frustrations of what appeared to be a hopeless situation.

In facing any new venture or seemingly impossible situation we can follow Peter's example, for we, too, have the Lord's word to believe and obey. Romans 10:17 tells us that "faith cometh by hearing, and hearing by the word of God." Then, like Peter, in taking the Lord at His word, we shall find that everything turns out for the best. Faith's reward is seeing the Lord turn failure into success and impossible problems into impressive solutions.

It's obvious how impressed Peter was with the turn of events he had witnessed. After wading through layers of fish, he fell down at Jesus' feet, imploring, "Depart from me; for I am a sinful man, O Lord" (Luke 5:8). We know from Scripture that Jesus Christ created all things and is in control of all things (John 1:3; Colossians 1:16,17; Hebrews 1:2,3). Just as He had prepared a great fish to swallow Jonah centuries before, so He was able to commandeer a large school of fish into Peter's net. Peter may not have known these theological facts when he fell down at Jesus' knees, but he surely understood that Jesus was Lord—all-powerful, all-knowing, and absolutely holy. And this correct view of Jesus enabled Peter to view himself correctly. In contrast to the sovereign, sinless, Son of God, Peter saw himself as a sinful man.

Peter wasn't the only one in history to blush with an overwhelming sense of sinfulness in the presence of the Lord. Job caught sight of the Lord near the end of his severe trials and confessed, "Behold, I am vile; what shall I answer thee? I will lay mine hand upon my mouth" (Job 40:4). Also, when Isaiah saw the Lord "sitting upon a throne, high and lifted up" (Isaiah 6:1), he cried out, "Woe is me! for I am undone; because I am a man of unclean lips, and I dwell in the midst of a people of unclean lips: for mine eyes have seen the King, the Lord of hosts" (verse 5).

By human standards, Job and Isaiah were anything but sinful men. And, indeed, by those same standards, Peter wasn't so bad either. As a matter of fact, the same thing could be said about us. But neither Job, Isaiah, Peter, nor any of us can measure up to the perfect righteousness of the Lord. As we perceive His perfection, we feel constrained to fall down before Him, as Peter did, and confess our sinfulness.

Our Lord didn't depart from Peter, for He had come to earth to save sinners, bring them into fellowship with Himself, and use them in His service. Peter must have been amazed at Jesus' response. "Fear not," Jesus said; "from henceforth thou shalt catch men" (verse 10).

The call to discipleship was clear. It was time for Peter, Andrew, James, and John to leave their full-time business to follow the Master. So, "when they had brought their ships to land, they forsook all, and followed him" (verse 11).

Do you realize what courage, dedication, and faith it took for Peter and his partners to leave everything behind and go with Jesus? At their feet lay the biggest catch of fish they had ever hauled in. What a price those fish would bring at the market! So they weren't just walking away from fish, they were walking away from big money! Furthermore, they were leaving behind their boats, their nets, their relatives, their homes, familiar surroundings, and an occupation that had been fairly good to them. But they had attached a greater value to following Jesus than to everything else, so with tremendous courage, dedication, and faith they placed their destinies in the hands of the Master. We may never be called upon to leave our homes, possessions, loved ones, and familiar surroundings for a life of service, but we are all called to serve the Master; and following Him should be our highest value.

As Peter walked along the shore, following Jesus, little did he realize what was involved in fishing for men, but he would learn. Slowly. Sometimes painfully. But he would surely learn!

3
Walking By Faith— On Water!

According to a certain story, a student of average ability and talent requested an entrance application of a very prestigious college known for its high academic standards and excellent programs. Upon receiving the application, the student began filling it out until he came to the self-analysis section. There he hesitated, noticing the question: "How do you rate your leadership ability? Exceptional ____ High ____ Average ____ Below Average ____." Feeling that he should be honest, the student put a check mark beside the "Below Average" option, then completed the application and mailed it, holding out little hope that the college would accept anyone with below average leadership. But, a few weeks later, he received a cordial acceptance letter from the registrar. "I am happy to inform you of your acceptance for enrollment in our college," the letter advised. "We received 3,000 applications, and yours was the only one that did not indicate exceptional leadership ability. We feel that all those exceptional leaders entering our college this fall will need a follower, so we shall look forward to your enrollment."

Today, there is certainly no lack of people who are impressed with their own abilities. They rush to disciple others before they themselves have been discipled. And they rush into the spotlight before spending adequate time in a quiet place learning to know the Lord better. What we desperately need in Christian circles is a willingness to follow the Lord and learn of Him before we assume leadership and presume to teach others. As the Apostle James advised, "My brethren, be not many masters [teachers], knowing that we shall receive the greater condemnation" (James 3:1).

Peter was humble enough to follow Jesus and to learn from Him how to fish for men. He watched as the Master drew all kinds of people to Himself. He saw Him reach out to the multitude with love, understanding, forgiveness, compassion, kindness, concern, and mercy. As Peter watched, Jesus cleansed a leper, healed a Roman centurion's servant, cured Peter's mother-in-law of a severe fever, cast out demons, forgave sins, made the lame to walk, healed a hemorrhaging woman, revived a comatose girl, restored sight to the blind and hearing to the deaf, assembled disciples, and fed 5,000 with just five bread rolls and two fish (Matthew 8—15).

But Peter's training involved far more than simply watching Jesus reach out to people in need. It also involved several lessons on trusting implicitly in Jesus Christ as the Son of God who is in control of every situation. After all, in the years to come Peter would face many desperate situations in which only a resolute confidence in Christ would see him through.

One of those situations is described in Matthew 14:22-33. Jesus had instructed His disciples to get into a boat and cross the Sea of Galilee while He stayed behind for awhile. It was evening, and He wanted to send away the 5,000 whom He had fed miraculously. So the disciples boarded their boat and cast off on what was to be an unforgettable adventure for them, and especially for Peter.

After dismissing the multitude, Jesus climbed to a secluded spot on a mountain and spent several hours in prayer. But while He prayed, His disciples panicked. During those hours, they had been bucking strong wind and high waves. They must have wondered if they would ever reach the opposite shore. There they were, several hours into a voyage that stretched only four miles from shore to shore, yet they had reached only the mid-point. Now, the wind and waves were doing their utmost to make the boat capsize. Furiously the wind whipped the sea into a swelling, rolling monster. While the boat pitched and tossed violently, the disciples must have hung on to the sides of the boat for the wildest, scariest ride of their lives. And they must have decided that it would end quickly in a mass drowning.

Do you wonder why the all-knowing Son of God allowed His followers to get into such a mess? Do you wonder why He allows us to get into some stormy situations? Can't He foresee these frantic situations and steer us around them, just as an airline navigator sees violent storms on his radar screen and changes the flight pattern to avoid them?

I get more than a little perturbed when I hear or read what some are teaching: "If you will just trust in Jesus as your Saviour, your problems will be over. With Jesus in control, everything will come up roses. No more unhappiness. No more loneliness. You will have health, prosperity, and happiness forever." The fact is, Jesus never promised His followers a platinum-coated, sunny road to Heaven. He said, "In the world ye shall have tribulation: but be of good cheer; I have overcome the world" (John 16:33).

Did you catch the significance of Jesus' words? "Tribulation?" Yes. But in the midst of tribulation, we can have "good cheer," because Jesus, our Lord, is the *overcomer*!

Peter and the other disciples needed to learn that in their service for Jesus Christ they would encounter plenty of storms. Trials, persecution, suffering, loneliness, disappointments, and hardship would dog their steps. Also, they needed to learn that Jesus' joy can pervade hard times. All it takes is the assurance that He, the overcomer, is in control of all things. Fishing for men would have to continue in bad weather as well as in good weather.

Knowing that His disciples were in big trouble, Jesus went to them "in the fourth watch of the night . . . walking on the sea" (Matthew 14:25). This was a spectacular demonstration of His control over the elements, but it was also a spectacular demonstration of His compassionate concern. We never lie beyond the reach of our Lord's knowledge, care, and power, although sometimes we forget this. Too often, we deal with our problems by following this advice:

When in trouble, when in doubt,
Run in circles, scream and shout.

It's far better, of course, to follow the advice Peter offered later in his life: "Casting all your care upon him; for he careth for you" (I Peter 5:7).

Have you ever taken a really close look at a very familiar psalm—Psalm 23? If you have, perhaps you have noticed how the Lord is referred to indirectly in the first three verses as "He." "*He* maketh me to lie down in green pastures; *he* leadeth me beside the still waters. *He* restoreth my soul: *he* leadeth me in the paths of righteousness for his name's sake." But there is a sudden shift in verse 4 to a direct relationship with the Lord, so that

27

in verses 4 and 5 the psalmist addresses the Lord as a close companion and protector. "*Thou* art with me; thy rod and thy staff they comfort me. *Thou* preparest a table before me in the presence of mine enemies: *thou* anointest my head with oil; my cup runneth over." The pivotal point on which the relationship swings from indirect to intimate is the first part of verse 4: "Yea, though I walk through the valley of the shadow of death." Before that point, everything was so comfortable: green pastures, placid waters, quiet paths. Then the valley of the shadow of death gripped the psalmist in its ominous, cold, clammy darkness, and he sensed deep down in his soul that he needed to draw closer to the Lord than ever before.

Haven't you known this experience? When everything was going smoothly—bills were all paid, health was good, and you were getting along well with the neighbors—you knew the Lord was your Shepherd, but you didn't sense a critical need to get really close to Him. Then, POW! Some crisis hit you like a cement truck, and you found yourself flat on your back. Then, looking up at the Lord, you implored, "Lord I need You now more than ever before. Please, help me."

Peter was going through a valley-of-the-shadow-of-death experience when Jesus approached the boat. At first, when he and the others saw Jesus walking on the water, they were terrified, supposing that they were looking at a ghost (Matthew 14:26). As if it weren't horrible enough to be trapped in a tempest, now they were confronted with what appeared to be a ghost. But Jesus immediately calmed their fear, saying, "Be of good cheer; it is I; be not afraid" (verse 27).

That was all Peter needed to hear. Now, in that valley-of-the-shadow-of-death experience he wanted to get as close to Jesus as he could get. "Lord, if it be thou, bid me come unto thee on the water," he called out.

"Come," Jesus invited.

The big fisherman climbed out of the boat, planted his feet on the water, and walked toward Jesus. This took enormous faith. Anyone with half a grain of common sense could have told Peter he couldn't walk on water. Water was meant for drinking, fishing, swimming, and boating, but it certainly wasn't meant for walking. But, then, Jesus had said, "Come," and that was enough for Peter.

When the Lord calls upon us to do something, we should never hesitate to do it, even if the assignment looks impossible. If we must have all the details spelled out for us before we step out of the boat, we'll never get anywhere. It's best to step out to do the impossible and let the Lord handle the insurmountable obstacles.

For a little while Peter made great progress in walking on the sea toward Jesus. But suddenly he shifted his attention from Jesus to the boisterous wind, became frightened, and started sinking. Desperately he shouted, "Lord, save me" (verse 30).

Immediately Jesus reached out and

caught Peter. "O thou of little faith, where-fore didst thou doubt?" He asked His drenched disciple (verse 31).

Peter was definitely a man of contrasts, wasn't he? One minute he showed gigantic faith in the Lord by getting out of the boat and walking on the water toward Him at His invitation. Then, the next minute, he took his eyes off Jesus, and sank in the water. I sup-pose we, too, have shown the same kind of contrast—faith one minute, doubt the next—and this is another reason why we see so much of ourselves in Peter.

A couple of challenging observations come to mind as I read Jesus' words, "O thou of little faith, wherefore didst thou doubt?" First, I find myself thinking about more than a few occasions when my adverse circum-stances were far less trying that Peter's, yet I failed to believe that the Lord was stronger than those circumstances. So I wonder, what must the Lord think of my paltry faith, since He gave Peter such a low rating on his! Then, I think about what could be accomplished if my faith and the faith of fellow Christians were greater. There is no doubt that if Peter had retained resolute faith in Jesus he could have walked on the water all the way to Jesus. He could have gone walking with Jesus back to the boat, or even to the shore two miles away.

As soon as Jesus and Peter got into the boat, the tempestuous storm stopped, and the sea-weary disciples worshiped Him, say-ing, "Of a truth thou art the Son of God" (verse 33). The tempest had served its purpose. Peter's faith had been tested, and Jesus had demonstrated His sovereign power to take care of His followers in even the most desperate circumstances. Peter would emerge from this dramatic incident with a stronger faith in his Master and a weaker confidence in himself. But other tests lay ahead.

In writing about Jesus' walking on the water toward the disciples' storm-tossed boat, Augustine commented: "He came treading the waves; and so he puts all the swelling tumults of life under his feet. Christians—why afraid?"

Yes, why do we fear and fail to maintain resolute faith in the Lord? He has pledged that He will never leave us nor forsake us (Hebrews 13:5). He has assured us in His Word that "we are more than conquerors through him" (Romans 8:37). And He has said, "Peace I leave with you, my peace I give unto you: . . . Let not your heart be troubled, neither let it be afraid" (John 14:27).

Obviously we live in perilous times. Hostile nations have the military capability of blasting our cities off the earth. Our children and grandchildren are exposed to a steady barrage of anti-Christian attitudes and opinions in spite of our best efforts to protect them. Unemployment, inflation, and other threatening situations surround us like the swelling waves that surrounded Peter. And just as Peter by faith sought the security of Jesus' presence, so we by faith try to keep our eyes on Jesus and step by step get closer to Him. But sometimes, like Peter, we take our eyes off the Lord and look fearfully at the turbulent conditions around us. That's when we would surely go under if it were not for the Lord's love and grace. He always reaches out and rescues us, asking, "Wherefore didst thou doubt?"

Peter surely learned from his experience, for he and the others in the boat worshiped Jesus as the Son of God. We, too, can learn from each experience we have with life's rough storms. We can see that the Son of God merits our abiding faith, for He can keep us safe and can tame even the most savage tempest.

4
A Firm Confession
Of Faith

Have you read the church ads in the Yellow Pages of your phone book? If not, let your fingers walk to church. I think you'll be amazed at the number and variety of churches your community includes. And perhaps you will wonder how many of those churches know Christ as Saviour. Obviously a person may claim religious affiliation without holding the conviction that Jesus Christ is the Son of God who died for our sins.

Many religious people are like the church member who was asked, "What do you believe about Jesus Christ?"

"I believe what my church believes," he replied.

"And what does your church believe?" the inquirer demanded.

"It believes what I believe," the church member countered.

"And just what is it that you and your church believe?" pressed the inquirer.

"We both believe the same thing," the church member explained.

Pretty shaky faith, wouldn't you say? It certainly isn't the kind of faith that honors Jesus Christ. Nor is it the kind of faith that Christ can bless in any tangible way.

One day, as Jesus and His disciples approached Caesarea Philippi, a city about 25 miles north of the Sea of Galilee, Jesus gave His disciples a brief but vitally important test on faith. Although it had only two questions, it effectively measured the strength of their belief in Jesus as Israel's Messiah and the Son of God.

The first question, recorded in Matthew 16:13, probed the disciples' knowledge of public opinion. Jesus asked: "Whom do men say that I the Son of man am?" Obviously, the disciples had picked up numerous comments from the multitudes who had followed Jesus on many occasions. They must have overheard people discussing what they thought of Jesus, the Preacher from Nazareth. After all, human nature is basically the same throughout history, and one phenomenon of human nature is that people like to find out what others think of some preacher, especially the newest preacher to arrive on the scene.

The disciples earned an "A" on the first part of their test, for they knew exactly what people were saying about Jesus. They answered in verse 14: "Some *say that thou art* John the Baptist; some, Elias [Elijah]; and others, Jeremias, or one of the prophets."

Interesting, isn't it, that Jesus had impressed onlookers and listeners in these different ways? Indeed there were striking similarities between Jesus and each of the persons He was mistaken for. His simple lifestyle and authoritative, straightforward preaching of repentance closely paralleled the lifestyle and preaching of the late John the Baptist. No wonder so many people felt that He was John, risen from the dead. And it is equally understandable that others mistook Him for Elijah. Jesus' miracles were certainly reminiscent of those performed so long ago by Elijah. And, after all, God had promised through Malachi: "Behold, I will send you Elijah the prophet before the coming of the great and dreadful day of the Lord" (Malachi 4:5). As for the Jeremiah identification, Jesus' deep compassion coupled with His warnings about sin and judgment must have convinced a segment of the population that He was Jeremiah. Still others were reluctant to assign a specific prophet's name to Jesus. They preferred to say simply that He was "one of the prophets."

Obviously, all of the identifications Jesus received from those who were favorable to His ministry were rather illustrious, but they were incorrect and inadequate. A correct concept of Jesus Christ involves far more than just a noble opinion of Him. If the disciples were simply in agreement with one of the popular views of Jesus, they certainly weren't ready for the major responsibility of preaching the good news about Him. So Jesus moved on to the second question in His test of their faith. "But whom say ye that I am?" He demanded (Matthew 16:15).

The disciples had heard the popular opinions. On the other hand, they had seen Jesus' miracles, which pronounced so clearly and forcefully that He was the Messiah and God's Son. Had the opinions of men molded their their concept of Jesus? Or, had the miracles molded their concept of Him?

In *The Supernaturalness of Christ* (page 125), author Wilbur M. Smith alludes to the purpose of Christ's miracles:

Christ's miracles had two fundamental objectives: first, that of helping broken, diseased, enslaved, handicapped men and women to obtain soundness of health again, freedom from demon-enslavement, hearing, sight, the ability to walk, etc., etc.; secondly, to glorify God in such a way that men would recognize that the One performing these miracles was indeed one sent by and approved by God.

Did the disciples recognize Jesus as one sent by and approved by God? Had Jesus' miracles up to this time fulfilled their second purpose, as Dr. Smith describes it? The answer is yes.

Peter didn't wait for the others to reply. Like a schoolboy with a correct answer and an uncontrollable urge to be the first to tell his teacher, Peter exclaimed: "Thou art the Christ, the Son of the living God" (verse 16). This was a confession of faith that would receive Jesus' commendation and form the foundation for Peter's preaching in years to come.

Jesus was elated. His Father's witness to His messiahship and deity had opened Peter's eyes and heart to the truth. Responding to Peter's confession, He declared, "Blessed art thou, Simon Barjona: for flesh and blood hath not revealed it unto thee, but my Father which is in heaven" (verse 17). Then, He made a pronouncement which has been the subject of much theological discussion:

"... thou art Peter, and upon this rock I will build my church; and the gates of hell shall not prevail against it. And I will give unto thee the keys of the kingdom of heaven: and whatsoever thou shalt bind on earth shall be bound in heaven: and whatsoever thou shalt loose on earth shall be loosed in heaven" (verses 18,19).

Two questions loom large in theological discussion regarding Jesus' pronouncement to Peter: 1) What is the "rock" on which Christ promised to build His church? and 2) What is meant by Peter's receiving "the keys of the kingdom of heaven''? These are important questions, crucial to our understanding of Peter's role in the history of the church.

In response to the first question, three interpretations are advanced. 1) The rock is Peter. 2) The rock is Peter's confession of faith in Christ as Messiah and the Son of God. 3) The rock is Jesus Christ.

The first of these interpretations has nothing to commend it to Bible-believing Christians, for it fails to distinguish between the two Greek words meaning *rock* in Matthew 16:18 and thereby makes Peter the foundation for Christ's church. The first word is *petros,* Peter's name; whereas the second is *petra,* the ''rock'' on which Christ would build His church.

The second interpretation has gained favorable acceptance among Bible-believing Christians because confession of Christ as God's Son and our Saviour is certainly foundational to belonging to Christ's church.

I prefer the third interpretation, though, believing that Jesus Christ is the Rock on which the church is being built. For one thing, *petros,* Peter's name, signifies ''a detached stone or boulder,'' whereas *petra* connotes ''a mass of live rock'' (*Abbot-Smith's Greek Lexicon of the New Testament*). Peter was a little rock, but Jesus Christ was and is a solid, invulnerable Rock. Also, several Scripture passages identify Jesus Christ as the church's foundation-rock. First Corinthians 3:11 states: ''For other foundation can no man lay than that is laid, which is Jesus Christ." Ephesians 2:20 indicates: "[Ye] are built upon the foundation of the apostles and prophets, Jesus Christ himself being the chief corner stone." And later in life Peter himself referred to Jesus Christ as "a living stone," "a chief corner stone," "the head of the corner, and a stone of stumbling, and a rock of offence" (see I Peter 2:4-8).

With Jesus Christ as the foundation-rock of the church and as its builder as well, it isn't hard to understand why "the gates of hell shall not prevail against it" (Matthew 16:18b). Satan and his demons may scheme, sneer, and strike the church, but they will never win the war. In the end, the church militant will be the church victorious.

Now, what did our Lord mean when He told Peter He would give him the keys of the kingdom of heaven? Perhaps the best answer to this question comes from asking another: What unlocks the kingdom of heaven so that sinners may enter? It is the preaching of the gospel, which is "the power of God unto salvation to every one that believeth; to the Jew first, and also to the Greek" (Romans 1:16). And a look at Peter's later life as an apostle reveals that he used preaching to unlock the kingdom of heaven for the Jews on the Day of Pentecost (Acts 2) and for the Gentiles in the home of Cornelius (Acts 10).

Peter was coming along well in his training for apostleship. Near Caesarea-Philippi, he had voiced his firm conviction that Jesus was the Messiah and the Son of God. Eventually, he would preach this conviction to thousands. But he still had a long way to go. He would still suffer lapses of faith and be afflicted occasionally with foot-in-mouth disease. He would be up and down. However, over the long haul divine grace would triumph, and Peter would emerge as a forceful preacher and a dynamic leader.

5
Preview Of Glory

Peter just keeps on showing us contrasting sides of his personality. No sooner had he confessed that Jesus was the Messiah and the Son of God than he was saying something really off-base. Matthew 16:21,22 carries the sad account:

"From that time forth began Jesus to shew unto his disciples, how that he must go unto Jerusalem, and suffer many things of the elders and chief priests and scribes, and be killed, and be raised again the third day. Then Peter took him, and began to rebuke him, saying, Be it far from thee, Lord: this shall not be unto thee."

Can you picture how Peter must have reacted to Jesus' prediction? As soon as Jesus mentioned that He would suffer and be killed, Peter probably drew himself up to his full height, folded his arms across his burly chest, furrowed his brow, and stared openmouthed at Jesus. Then, he walked up to Jesus, steered Him away from the rest of the disciples, and lowered the boom. The fuse attached to Peter's time-bomb temper had been ignited, and when the sparks reached the end of the fuse, the bomb exploded into a volley of fiery words. Like a burst of sharp, cutting shrapnel, Peter's rebuke bombarded Jesus: "BE IT FAR FROM THEE, LORD: THIS SHALL NOT BE UNTO THEE."

Once again, Peter had said the wrong thing. Although he had recognized Jesus as the Messiah and the Son of God, he certainly didn't recognize the will of God when it was spelled out to him by none other than his Lord. Like so many Jews to whom the gospel would be preached, Peter assumed that the cross could have no place in God's plans for the Messiah. How could the King of all kings, Israel's hope personified, come to such an inglorious end? Wouldn't all the hopes and dreams of national identity, freedom, peace, prosperity, and spiritual revival fade away if the Messiah died? These questions must have gnawed at Peter.

We Christians have an advantage over Peter, of course, because he couldn't pull out a pocket New Testament and read there that the blood of Christ is the basis on which

God will restore Israel to Himself and the kingdom to Israel. For example, here are two New Testament passages which show how Jesus Christ's shed blood is foundational to Israel's redemption and participation in Messiah's kingdom.

"And so all Israel shall be saved: as it is written, There shall come out of Sion the Deliverer, and shall turn away ungodliness from Jacob: For this is my covenant unto them, when I shall take away their sins" (Romans 11:26,27).

"For finding fault with them, he saith, Behold the days come, saith the Lord, when I will make a new covenant with the house of Israel and with the house of Judah . . . But Christ being come an high priest of good things to come, by a greater and more perfect tabernacle, not made with hands, that is to say, not of this building, Neither by the blood of goats and calves, but by his own blood he entered in once into the holy place, having obtained eternal redemption for us. For if the blood of bulls and of goats, and the ashes of an heifer sprinkling the unclean, sanctifieth to the purifying of the flesh: How much more shall the blood of Christ, who through the eternal Spirit offered himself without spot to God, purge your conscience from dead works to serve the living God? And for this cause he is the mediator of the new testament, that by means of death, for the redemption of the transgressions that were under the first testament, they which are called might receive the promise of eternal inheritance" (Hebrews 8:8; 9:11-15).

We also know from New Testament passages that Jesus' shed blood is the basis upon which we have redemption and the privilege of having a place in His church. For example:

"Take heed . . . to feed the church of God, which he hath purchased with his own blood" (Acts 20:28).

"In whom we have redemption through his blood, the forgiveness of sins, according to the riches of his grace" (Ephesians 1:7).

"Giving thanks unto the Father, which hath made us meet to be partakers of the inheritance of the saints in light: Who hath delivered us from the power of darkness, and hath translated us into the kingdom of his dear Son: In whom we have redemption through his blood, even the forgiveness of sins: Who is the image of the invisible God . . . And he is the head of the body, the church" (Colossians 1:12-18).

But Peter did know who Jesus was, didn't

he? And he should have known enough Old Testament teaching to realize that Israel's Messiah would suffer and die for sin. If he had read only Isaiah 53:6,7, he should have known that the Messiah was destined to die. The Prophet Isaiah had declared:

> "All we like sheep have gone astray; we have turned every one to his own way; and the Lord hath laid on him the iniquity of us all. He was oppressed, and he was afflicted, yet he opened not his mouth: he is brought as a sheep to the slaughter, and as a sheep before her shearers is dumb, so he openeth not his mouth."

So Peter's rebuke of the Lord Jesus was certainly an unfounded attack on the will of God and an awesome display of ignorance.

It was also ridiculous that Peter addressed Jesus as "Lord" while telling Him off and dictating to Him. But it is often the way of Jesus' followers to call Him Lord and reject His plans. Apparently there lies within even the best of us an ego that occasionally rebels against the Lord and orders Him off the throne so we can sit there and do a better job of ruling.

Peter's name, "Simon," means *who hears,* but he certainly wasn't hearing very well when Jesus predicted His suffering and crucifixion. If he had been listening properly, he would have heard Jesus say that He would be raised again the third day (Matthew

16:21). But because Peter had his hearing turned down too low, all he could think about was an abrupt end to Jesus' life. And that dreadful prospect upset him terribly.

Now, here's a harsh, sad fact. Peter was upset because he feared he was going to lose everything by following Jesus to such a disastrous end. Why, if he had known in the beginning that Jesus was going to die on a cross, he would have stayed in Bethsaida and maintained his fishing business!

Jesus knew full well that Peter's spirited objection to the way of the cross was simply a smoke screen to hide the resentment that was smoldering in his heart. Turning abruptly away from Peter, Jesus ordered, "Get thee behind me, Satan: for thou art an offence unto me: for thou savourest not the things that be of God, but those that be of men" (verse 23).

Peter was guilty of two sins in trying to deter Jesus from going to the cross. There was, first of all, the sin of playing into Satan's hands. Satan wanted to hinder Jesus in His work of redemption. He had tempted Jesus once to bypass the cross and receive the kingdoms of the world in return for bowing down before him and worshiping him (Matthew 4:8,9). He realized that Jesus' death on the cross would bring the curtain down on his diabolical drama of sinister crimes against God and man. He knew that the cross would provide man's only way of escape from his kingdom of darkness and despair. Secondly, Peter was guilty of pursuing the kind of reasoning that is characteristic of men who reject God. His reasoning was self-centered instead of Christ-centered. He didn't want to hear about suffering and death; he wanted to hear about all the good things that were in store for Jesus and His followers.

Is it any wonder Jesus rebuked Peter, calling him an "offence"? The Greek word for "offence" is *skandalon,* which means a *stumblingblock.* In trying to block Jesus' path to the cross, Peter, whose name means *rock,* had become an obstruction like a big rock in the middle of a road. Before Peter would be ready to preach about the cross, he would need to know experientially the meaning of the cross. He would need to undergo a philosophical metamorphosis in which he would assign the highest values to self-denial and sacrifice for the sake of Jesus Christ. So Jesus concluded His rebuke of Peter with a lesson on cross-bearing.

If any man would follow Jesus, he must deny himself, take up his cross, and follow Him, Jesus explained (Matthew 16:24). Rejecting Him in favor of "the good life," as the world defines it in terms of possessions and self-centered pleasures, is certain to lead to a wasted life and to a disastrous afterlife (verses 25,26). Jesus explained further that a commitment to Him that welcomes self-denial and sacrifice for His sake leads to fulfillment and eternal reward (verses 25b,27). Then Jesus ended the lesson on a high note. He encouraged Peter and the others to look beyond the cross to the glory He would manifest in returning to the earth from Heaven to establish His kingdom. And He promised that some of His disciples would not die before catching a glimpse of that glory (verse 28).

Peter didn't have to wait long for the fulfillment of Jesus' promise. Just six days later, he, James, and John accompanied Jesus to the summit of a high mountain. There they were dazzled by a manifestation of Jesus' glory. Matthew 17:2 states that Jesus "was transfigured before them: and his face did shine as the sun, and his raiment was white as light."

The brilliant glory which set Jesus' face aglow and made his garment brighter than the sun emanated from within Him. For a brief time the radiant glory of Jesus' deity burst through His humanity. It was a sight Peter would never forget. Years later, in writing his second epistle, he recalled the event, saying: "For we have not followed cunningly devised fables, when we made known unto you the power and coming of our Lord Jesus Christ, but were eyewitnesses of his majesty" (II Peter 1:16).

There was a side attraction on the Mount of Transfiguration. Moses and Elijah appeared and talked with the Lord Jesus. Luke 9:31 tells us they spoke to Him about "his decease which he should accomplish at Jerusalem." Interesting, isn't it, that the representative of the Old Testament law and the representative of the Old Testament prophets understood clearly that Jesus would die on the cross. Even though Peter had tried to push all thoughts of the cross far from his thinking and that of his Master, Heaven's visitors to the mount had Jesus' impending crucifixion uppermost in their thinking. It's also interesting that later on, after Jesus had died and risen from the dead, He used the Old Testament's books of Moses and those of the prophets to convince two disciples on the Emmaus Road that He, the Messiah, died and rose again according to God's prophetic plan (Luke 24:13-15,25-27).

Many Bible teachers believe that Moses and Elijah will put in another appearance on the earth, and they will do so in the tribulation period before Jesus Christ returns to earth to smite His enemies and inaugurate His thousand-year rule. Revelation 11 speaks of two powerful witnesses who will prophesy on the earth for three and a half years of the tribulation period and, although the chapter does not name these witnesses, it does describe their ministries. According to verse 6, they "have power to shut heaven, that it rain not in the days of their prophecy: and have power over waters to turn them to blood, and to smite the earth with all plagues, as often as they will." Isn't the withholding of rain for three and a half years reminiscent of Elijah's prophetic career? And isn't the turning of water to blood and the smiting of the earth with plagues reminiscent of Moses' activity in Egypt before the exodus? It does seem plausible, therefore, that Elijah and Moses will witness on the earth prior to Christ's Second Coming.

To say the least, when Peter saw Moses and Elijah on the mountain, he was awe-struck. But he wasn't speechless. He exclaimed: "Lord, it is good for us to be here: if thou wilt, let us make here three tabernacles; one for thee, and one for Moses, and one for Elias" (Matthew 17:4).

Peter was still speaking when a bright cloud—perhaps the shekinah glory cloud—engulfed the mountaintop, and God commanded: "This is my beloved Son, in whom I am well pleased; hear ye him" (verse 5). This, too, was something Peter never forgot. In that same passage in II Peter, he wrote that Jesus Christ "received from God the Father honour and glory, when there came such a voice to him from the excellent glory, This is my beloved Son, in whom I am well pleased. And this voice which came from heaven we heard when we were with him in the holy mount" (1:17,18).

The voice from Heaven directed Peter's attention to Jesus Christ, for Peter had made the mistake of equating Him with great spiritual leaders. The fact of the matter is, Jesus Christ ranks far above even the most righteous mortals, for He is Deity. As such, He ought to be worshiped exclusively and be heeded implicitly.

While it is legitimate to honor our Christian leaders, we must never idolize them. Even the most widely acclaimed Christian leader is just a mortal and a sinner saved by the grace of God. Furthermore, Christian leaders who are devoted to Jesus Christ are quick to ask would-be admirers to pass all the bouquets up to Heaven to the One who deserves them.

I have heard that a famous pastor of a few generations ago became ill on a Sunday morning and summoned his brother to preach for him. Upon seeing the virtually unknown brother in the pulpit of their church, many disappointed parishioners left their pews and headed for the exits. They were stopped in their tracks, though, by the guest preacher's words. "All who came to church today to worship my brother may leave, while all who came to worship Jesus Christ will remain to do so." Let us never forget that Jesus alone merits our worship. As the hymn says, "No mortal can with Him compare."

Peter needed to focus his attention on Jesus Christ exclusively for another reason. He had been called to serve and not to sit indefinitely on the mountain reveling in a high spiritual experience. At the foot of the mountain were people with heavy cares and difficult problems. He had been blessed with a glimpse of Jesus' glory, and he had been blessed by seeing and hearing two foremost leaders from the pages of Israel's history, but it was time to leave all that behind and rub shoulders with a mass of humanity that desperately needed to be ministered to.

Peter had received important teaching. He had been taught to accept self-denial and sacrifice as integral factors in following

Jesus Christ. He had also been taught to reject the temptation to remain aloof from the hurts and heartaches of humanity while preferring to bask forever in a high spiritual experience. Are these lessons we, too, need in these critical times? If so, we can benefit from these challenging words by David Brainerd, dedicated missionary to the Indians in early America:

"I cared not where or how I lived, or what hardships I went through, so that I could gain souls to Christ. While I was asleep I dreamed of these things, and when I awoke the first thing I thought of was this great work. All my desires were for the conversion of the heathen, and all my hope was in God."

6
A Cowardly Denial

It's human to minimize the faults of relatives, friends, and others who mean a great deal to us. We sometimes go to almost any extreme to gloss over their obvious faults. Whitney N. Seymour has underscored this tendency in a story about a proud, prominent family. According to Seymour, the children of this family decided to give their aging father a book of their family's history. So they hired a biographer, and warned him of one problem—Uncle Willie, who had gone to the electric chair for murder.

The biographer assured the family that he would handle the situation discreetly. "I'll just say that Uncle Willie occupied a chair of applied electronics at one of our leading government institutions. He was attached to his position by the strongest of ties. His death came as a true shock."

Of course, once in a while someone emerges as an exception to the tendency to gloss over faults and imperfections. Oliver Cromwell, Lord Protector of the Commonwealth of England from 1653 to 1658, was such a person. When he was having his portrait painted, he noticed that the artist had not included a wart on his face in the painting. "Paint me as I am," Cromwell demanded, "wart and all."

In His Word, God has painted a portrait of Peter—wart and all. We have already seen a few flaws in Peter's character—chips in the "rock," so to speak—but we have learned that God was working in the life of this great man. Eventually Peter would become a highly disciplined, godly, and powerful leader in the church. However, before we take a close-up look at him in that commendable role, we must see him at his worst as he denies Christ three times in a brief span of time.

Peter had every reason to stand up for Jesus. Not only had he seen the glory of Jesus Christ on the Mount of Transfiguration, but he had also received a firm command from God to fix his attention on Jesus Christ. Then, after leaving the mountain, he followed Jesus in a journey that led inevitably to Jerusalem and the crucifixion. Along the way, Peter saw Jesus do great things. He saw Him free a frenzied child from a demon's horrible clutches. He watched

Him heal multitudes of men and women. He witnessed the cleansing of ten lepers. He saw Jesus lift little children in His arms and bless them. He saw Him raise Lazarus from the dead, give sight to blind beggars, and introduce Zacchaeus, a tax-collector, to the joy of salvation. And he saw Him ride triumphantly into Jerusalem as Israel's Messiah-King. All that Peter saw during that journey should have given him more than enough stamina to stand up for Jesus, but somehow Peter buckled under pressure and denied his Lord. However, we too have seen Jesus do marvelous things and can remember times when we buckled under pressure and denied Him.

That journey was also filled with wide-open opportunities for Peter to listen to Jesus' words—clear, compassionate, powerful, life-giving words. Unlike the hollow-sounding religious leaders of the day, Jesus communicated in a manner that gripped hearts and flooded the minds of receptive listeners with understanding, hope, and peace. So powerful were His words, that whenever the incredulous scribes, Pharisees, and Sadducees tried to trip Him up in His statements, Jesus turned the tables on them by confounding them and exposing their ignorance. Yes, Peter had heard enough wise teaching from Jesus to give him more than adequate reason to stand up for Him. But somehow he failed.

Again, we must remind ourselves that we are much like Peter. We, too, have had a great deal of exposure to Jesus' teachings but at times have failed to stand up for Him.

Six days after entering Jerusalem and just one day before the crucifixion, Jesus gathered His disciples together in an upper room for the Passover observance. Interestingly, the Passover Feast required the eating of a roast lamb—an unblemished lamb—in commemoration of the first Passover, when every Hebrew family in Egypt smeared the blood of an unblemished lamb on the doorposts, roasted the lamb, and ate it (Exodus 12:1-11). On that first Passover night, the Lord *passed over* every household displaying the blood of a Passover lamb. But the Lord smote the firstborn in every household not identified by the blood of a Passover lamb on their doorposts. This was His final judgment on Egypt which brought about the Hebrews' deliverance from slavery in Egypt.

The symbolism in all of this is clear. Jesus Christ was the unblemished Lamb of God. The Passover lamb He and His disciples ate in the upper room pictured Him. On the next day, He would shed His blood for the sins of the whole world, so that all who would believe on Him as Saviour would be sheltered by His blood from condemnation and be delivered from sin's slavery. Undoubtedly Peter didn't understand this symbolism when Jesus observed the Passover with him and the others, but later on he understood it. He wrote in I Peter 1:19 that we are redeemed "with the precious blood of Christ, as of a lamb without blemish and without spot.''

During the Passover Supper, Jesus showed Peter and the other disciples that He loved them. John 13:4,5 tells us that He arose from supper, removed His garments, clothed Himself with a towel, poured water into a basin, and began washing His disciples' feet. It was customary for a household servant to perform this service, but none was present, and the disciples weren't about to stoop to such a low level of servitude. They had big plans for themselves. As a matter of fact, Luke 22:24 indicates they were arguing among themselves about which of them should be V.I.P.s in Jesus' kingdom.

The disciples could hardly wait for the opportunity to occupy prominent positions in Jesus' kingdom. Their sights were set so high that they failed to see the lowly ministry needing to be performed right then and there—the ministry of bathing hot, tired feet. It is Christlike to seize whatever opportunities God gives us now, whether they are great or small, and to do them humbly as unto Him. If we refuse a task God gives us because we consider it to be beneath us, there is no reason to think He will give us a more prominent task later. Let's look around for some humble task God wants us to perform for the sake of others. It may be serving in the nursery, delivering flowers to the sick, raking leaves or shoveling snow for the elderly, painting Sunday School classrooms, preparing the church's bulletin, ushering, tidying up after a fellowship dinner, or any number of other unpretentious ministries which can do so much good and gain God's approval.

Peter resisted the Lord's efforts at washing his feet. "Lord, dost thou wash my feet?" he asked (John 13:6).

It was inconceivable to Peter's way of thinking that the holy Son of God should perform such a menial service. Apparently, Peter wasn't acting in a rebellious manner; he just felt strongly that Jesus' washing his feet was not the kind of thing a soon-to-be-crowned king should do. His deep respect for Jesus made him resist Jesus' efforts at washing his feet.

"What I do thou knowest not now; but thou shalt know hereafter," Jesus replied (verse 7).

Without asking Jesus to explain what He meant, Peter remonstrated, "Thou shalt never wash my feet" (verse 8).

Jesus told Peter, "If I wash thee not, thou hast no part with me" (verse 8b).

What did Jesus mean? He was telling Peter that only those whose sins are washed away belong to Him.

Peter didn't understand the symbolism behind Jesus' words, but he certainly wanted to belong to Jesus, so his whole attitude changed instantly. Instead of bristling with resistance to Jesus' offer to wash his feet, suddenly he wanted Jesus to give him a whole bath. He asked Jesus, "Lord, not my feet only, but also my hands and my head" (verse 9). It was as though he were saying,

"Lord, if it takes getting washed by you to belong to you, then wash me from head to toe."

Wasn't this just like Peter? So quick to say one thing, only to have to change his tune a few moments later. Often his heart spoke before his head had a chance to soak up some good theology. And I suppose it's sometimes the same with us—we mean well, but later enlightenment shows us where we were wrong in our impetuous words or actions.

Jesus had more to say to Peter. "He that is washed needeth not save to wash his feet, but is clean every whit: and ye are clean, but not all." That last part of Jesus' statement referred to Judas, who would betray him (verse 11). Judas had never been washed clean. He had never experienced Jesus' forgiveness. But Peter and the rest had experienced Jesus' forgiveness because they believed in Him. They belonged to Him. Nevertheless, they were not perfect. They would commit sins occasionally and therefore require cleansing from the Lord.

In first-century Palestine, the streets and roads were dusty and sandy. A person who took a bath at the public baths would get his feet dirty as he walked home. Upon reaching his house, he would simply wash his feet. He certainly would not go back to the public baths and wash his entire body again. Even so, a believer in Christ has been washed thoroughly from his sins. He is clean all over, and he belongs to Jesus Christ forever. But, as he walks through life, he sins occasionally; his feet get dirty, if you will, and he needs the restorative cleansing referred to in I John 1:9: "If we confess our sins, he is faithful and just to forgive us our sins, and to cleanse us from all unrighteousness." He certainly doesn't need to be saved all over again.

As Jesus had pointed out, Peter didn't understand the spiritual significance of the washing in the upper room, but he would understand later. Jesus was thinking about Peter's denial of Him which would occur that very night. That denial would not cause forfeiture of salvation, but it would interrupt Peter's fellowship with Jesus Christ and require restorative cleansing.

At the close of the Passover Supper, Jesus instituted the ordinance of communion, admonishing His followers to partake of the bread and cup in remembrance of Him. Then, when they had sung a hymn, they departed for the Mount of Olives.

As they were leaving, Jesus announced the tragic news that His disciples would be offended because of Him and would desert Him that very night (Matthew 26:31).

It wasn't received well by Peter. Jumping to his own defense, he insisted: "Though all men shall be offended because of thee, yet will I never be offended" (verse 33).

But Jesus was not impressed with Peter's self-confidence. He assured Peter: "Verily, I say unto thee, That this night, before the cock crow, thou shalt deny me thrice" (verse 34).

This really irked Peter. Didn't Jesus know that he was a strong, self-reliant, brave man? "Though I should die with thee, yet will I not deny thee," Peter bragged. And his braggadocio sparked the other disciples' pride, so that they, too, boasted that they would follow Jesus to His death.

Self-confidence is a poor substitute for confidence in God. Anyone who thinks he is strong enough or smart enough to serve Christ effectively without relying on God's power is headed for disaster. "Let him that thinketh he standeth, take heed lest he fall," the Bible warns. At Ai, the soldiers of Israel suffered an embarrassing defeat because they were self-confident. And Samson experienced disgrace and enslavement at the hands of the Philistines when he boasted that he would get up and shake them off as he had at other times. One big problem, though; he didn't realize the Lord had departed from him, leaving him to the sad consequences of his foolish pride.

If only Peter had learned something from those Old Testament episodes. Unfortunately, he just had to learn the hard way. Jesus knew this and informed Peter: "Satan hath desired to have you, that he may sift you as wheat: But I have prayed for thee, that thy faith fail not: and when thou art converted, strengthen thy brethren" (Luke 22:31,32).

What Jesus did for Peter in praying for him He also does for each of us. This assures us of victory in the Christian life. Sure, we will sin at times, but our Lord will never give up on us. His prayers for us will prevail. First John 2:1 exhorts us not to sin but informs us that, when we commit a sin, Jesus Christ pleads our case in Heaven. Along this same line, Hebrews 7:24,25 notifies us that Jesus Christ, as our high priest in Heaven, intercedes for us.

It was getting late when Jesus and His disciples reached the garden of Gethsemane on the side of the Mount of Olives. He left most of them at a spot in the garden, but took Peter, James, and John with Him to a place deeper in the garden. Then, He told the three to stay where they were and to watch and pray while He prayed nearby (Matthew 26:36-38; Luke 22:39-41).

Peter had been wrong in boasting self-confidently of his undying loyalty to Jesus Christ. Now, he was wrong in another matter: he failed to watch and pray while his Master agonized in prayer only a short distance away. While Jesus was wrestling in prayer over the grim prospect of dying on a cross as our sin-bearer, Peter and his two companions fell asleep. Perhaps they had tried very hard to stay awake and pray, but it had been a long, hard day. Gradually, their eyelids had become heavier and heavier until they closed.

After awhile, Jesus returned to the spot where He had left His three disciples. Finding them asleep, He said to Peter, "What, could ye not watch with me one hour? Watch and pray, that ye enter not into temptation: the spirit indeed is willing, but the flesh is weak'' (Matthew 26:40,41).

We can't condone the failure of Peter, James, and John to watch and pray, but neither can we cast stones at them. Haven't you and I learned by experience how hard it is to persevere in a spiritual endeavor when we are physically worn out? Perhaps you can recall coming home from work really dragged out but fully intending to go to Prayer Meeting after catching 40 post-supper winks in your favorite chair. Somehow those 40 winks turned into 400 winks. When you woke up, you couldn't believe how late it was—too late to go to Prayer Meeting. Or, can you recall a December 31st when you resolved to have your morning devotions every day of the new year? On January 1st you slipped out of bed half an hour earlier than usual and spent thirty minutes reading the Bible and praying. On January 2 you got up half an hour early again and had your quiet time with the Lord. January 3rd didn't go quite as well. Somehow the bed covers seemed heavier than usual—hard to throw off—and they seemed warmer, too. So you arose only fifteen minutes early and squeezed in a brief prayer and the reading of three verses of Scripture between a hot shower and a cup of coffee. January 4th was worse still; only a brief prayer between the shower and the coffee. By January 5th you were back into the previous year's routine, getting out of bed only in time for a shower and a cup of coffee before heading out the door to go to work. Yes, we had better not cast stones at Peter, James, and John, because we, too, know that "the spirit indeed is willing, but the flesh is weak."

Again, Jesus left His three disciples and prayed intensely, only to return and find them sleeping once more (Matthew 26:43). A third time, He prayed and returned to the sleeping trio. This time He told them: "Sleep on now, and take your rest: behold, the hour is at hand, and the Son of man is betrayed into the hands of sinners. Rise, let us be going: behold, he is at hand that doth betray me" (verses 45,46). Peter's opportunity of sharing the burden of prayer with Jesus was over. He had failed to give Jesus empathetic companionship at a desperately critical time. But another failure would emerge soon, and it would bring Peter to the lowest point of his life.

Suddenly Jesus' words were interrupted by the loud, discordant noises of clanking armor, jangling swords, banging clubs, and angry shouts. Soldiers and temple officers carrying torches and lanterns, swords and clubs, had arrived to arrest Jesus. And Judas, the betrayer, led the pack. With a hypocritical kiss, he identified Jesus for the arrestors.

Peter must have felt that an opportunity had arrived to compensate for his previous failures. He would show Jesus that he really was loyal to Him and would follow Him to the death! Leaping to Jesus' defense, the big, blustery fisherman swung his sword wildly. But he was accustomed to handling a net and not a sword. Consequently, his aim was bad. He chopped off the right ear of Malchus, a servant of the high priest.

I suppose if Peter had kept swinging that sword he would have inflicted heavy damage, such as five ears, thirteen torches, eight lanterns, sixteen branches, and four toes—his own. However, Jesus stepped into the melee, ordered Peter to "put up again thy sword into his place," explaining that those who live by the sword shall perish with the sword. He further explained that He could summon more than twelve legions of angels for His defense, but He would not because it was time for Him to go to the cross.

I find Peter's behavior in Gethsemane very interesting. He had failed to stay awake and pray with Jesus, as Jesus had instructed, but he wasted no time in rushing to Jesus' defense, even though Jesus hadn't asked him to do so. I guess Peter was a lot like us in this respect, too, because we often find it easier to plunge headlong into frenzied activity, which we call "Christian service," than to spend time in quiet fellowship with our Lord. However, getting immersed in busyness at church is no substitute for getting to know Christ better through prayer and Bible meditation, especially when we take on more jobs than He gives us. To be sure, He wants our fellowship rather than the sacrifice of a busy, burned-out life.

If you have been noticing Peter's most serious failures on the road to his biggest failure—the denial of Jesus Christ—you have observed that the first of these was self-confidence. He boasted that he would never forsake his Lord. Then, he failed to watch and pray in obedience to the Lord's command to do so. Next, he jumped into a frenzied flurry of fighting to repel Jesus' enemies. He soon learned that Jesus didn't approve of this. Now, as the story unfolds further, you will see another of Peter's failures. Matthew 26:58 points it out. As the soldiers led Jesus away, Peter "followed him afar off unto the high priest's palace." As you know, when Jesus had called Peter into full-time discipleship, He had said, "Follow me." Following afar off was not the kind of discipleship that honored Him. Apparently, what was uppermost in Peter's thinking was the tragedy of unfulfilled kingdom dreams. Now that everything seemed to be coming to a disastrous end for Jesus and His disciples, Peter must have reasoned that it wouldn't be smart to follow Jesus closely. Someone might recognize him and turn him over to the authorities.

Having gained entrance into the courtyard of the high priest's palace, where Jesus was put on trial, Peter warmed himself at a fire. But it soon got really hot for Peter, because a servant girl asked him: "Art not thou also one of this man's disciples?"

"I am not," Peter insisted (John 18:17).

Peter had denied his Lord once.

Likely fearing that he was easily recognized by the fire's light, Peter moved away toward the palace's porch. But another servant girl, a relative of Malchus, whose ear Peter had sliced off in the garden of Gethsemane, stopped him dead in his tracks. She pointed him out to the soldiers and onlookers by the fire. "This fellow was also with Jesus of Nazareth," she testified (Matthew 26:71).

"I do not know the man," Peter shouted (Matthew 26:72).

He had denied his Lord twice.

About an hour later, another person approached Peter. Within earshot of the soldiers, he looked Peter square in the eye and accused: "Surely thou also art one of them; for thy speech betrayeth thee" (verse 73). Peter's Galilean accent had given him away.

Calling down Heaven's judgment upon him if he were lying, Peter yelled, "I know not the man" (verse 74).

He had denied his Lord three times. And immediately the distinct, accusing crowing of a rooster pierced the cold night air. Then, as Jesus was led out of the palace and through the courtyard by his captors, He looked at Peter. It was a look that penetrated Peter's soul and made him feel the full weight of his guilt. It sent cold shivers down his spine. It jolted his memory. Peter remembered Jesus' prediction that he would deny Him three times before the rooster crowed.

It had been a bad night, an infamous night. Peter hurried out of the courtyard, choking back his tears. Then, somewhere in a lonely place and surrounded by the cold dusky dawn, he wept bitterly.

Surely there isn't a Christian anywhere who cannot identify with Peter in his denial of the Saviour and in the deep regret he felt afterwards. We have all denied our Lord at one time or another and in one way or another. Whether it was overt or covert, the denial brought us into a miserable state of heart and mind, and the heavens seemed like brass until we sought and received the Lord's forgiveness. Perhaps the denial took the form of a temper flare-up against a non-Christian neighbor. The harsh, angry words gave the neighbor the impression that his angry assailant was anything but a Christian. Or, perhaps the denial was communicated at an office party through behavior unbecoming to a follower of Christ. If it had not been for our Lord's far-reaching grace and inexhaustible love, we would never have recovered. But He who knows our weaknesses also heals our hurts. He does not despise a broken and contrite heart (Psalm 51:17). So He drew us back into the circle of His love, assured us of His forgiveness and encouraged us to serve Him with renewed devotion.

As we shall see, the Lord who had prayed for Peter was not about to cast him aside. The master Potter would mend the broken vessel and continue to shape it to His glory.

7
Restored

Peter's activities and whereabouts for the three days which separated his denial and Jesus' resurrection are shrouded in mystery. There is no clear indication in Scripture that he lingered near the cross on the first of those three days, although John stood by the cross. A few commentators, though, believe on the basis of Peter's precise description of the crucifixion in I Peter 2:20-24 that he watched from a distance. We can only surmise that by the end of the third day he had sought out John for comfort, because we do know Peter and John were together when word reached them early in the morning that the body of Jesus was missing from the tomb (John 20:1-3).

Wherever Peter spent those three days, he

must have been feeling tremendously lonely. Probably he passed the time silently and sullenly. We can well imagine that the dark days and starless nights were matched by Peter's mood—dark and desolate. It must have been the most despondent period of his life. Usually so quick to speak, likely he sat in stony silence for hours, opening his mouth only to emit heavy sighs or to ask himself the accusing, painful question, "Why did I deny the Lord?"

Peter was bound to recover, though. Had not the Lord foretold that he would? Before the denial, He had told Peter that He had prayed for him because Satan desired him. And He had promised that he would be restored and given an opportunity to strengthen the other disciples. The story of how that restoration came about is one of the most tender, compelling stories of the Bible.

The sun had just barely peeked over the eastern horizon when Mary and other women carrying burial spices arrived at Jesus' tomb. But Mary Magdalene left in a hurry when the group discovered that the body was missing. While the others lingered at the tomb, an angel appeared to them and announced that Jesus had risen from the dead. "But go your way, tell his disciples and Peter that he goeth before you into Galilee: there shall ye see him, as he said unto you," the angel instructed (Mark 16:7).

Does it seem strange that Peter was singled out in this way? Not at all. The risen Lord had Peter on His heart, just as He has each of us on His heart, even though we fail Him. Lovingly, patiently, He reaches out to us and draws us back to Himself.

Mary Magdalene was exhausted when she found Peter and John, for she had run all the way from the tomb. Gasping for breath, she told them, "They have taken away the Lord out of the sepulchre, and we know not where they have laid him" (John 20:2). She didn't have to say any more. Peter and John took off running toward the tomb.

Being lighter of foot, John arrived first. Stooping down, he looked into the tomb and saw the linen grave clothes lying intact. But he didn't enter. Then Peter arrived and proved in a hurry that he was still the same old Peter, at least in one respect: he was still impetuous. He rushed past John and entered the tomb, where he looked closely at the grave clothes, noticing especially the head wrapping, unwound and by itself. It was obvious that no one had unwrapped the burial clothes, and yet the body was gone!

Soon, John joined Peter in the tomb, and believed when he saw the head wrapping lying by itself—in place and undisturbed. Peter, on the other hand, left, "wondering in himself at that which was come to pass" (Luke 24:12).

Later that same day, the risen Lord appeared to Peter (Luke 24:34; I Corinthians 15:5), but the Scriptures do not disclose any details of this meeting. We can only conjecture that the Lord met privately with Peter at this time to spare him the embarrassment that might have accompanied a first-time resurrection appearance to him in the presence of the other disciples. It was best to settle family matters in a one-to-one manner.

In the evening, Jesus met with His disciples in the upper room. The disciples had bolted the doors because they feared the Jews might try to apprehend them. But locked doors were no obstacle to Jesus. Suddenly, He stood among His frightened men and said, "Peace be unto you" (John 20:19).

Thomas wasn't in the upper room on that resurrection day, so he wasn't persuaded by the testimony of the other disciples that Jesus had risen from the dead. However, eight days later, Jesus appeared again to His disciples in the upper room. This time Thomas was present, and after touching Jesus' wounded hands and side, he believed (verses 26-28).

The biggest, most important meeting of all, as far as Peter's restoration was concerned, took place at the Sea of Tiberias in Galilee. John 21:3 tells us that Peter informed the six disciples who were with him that he was going fishing. It was a good idea, they felt, so they replied, "We also go with thee."

I wonder if Peter had grown tired of waiting for Jesus to show up in Galilee as He had promised. Or did he suppose it would never be the same again as far as following Jesus and fishing for men were concerned? Maybe he thought he would soon have to return to the fishing trade and therefore should get in some practice. In any case, he and the rest hopped into a boat—perhaps a rented or borrowed boat—and headed for the fish.

It was like old times, the way things were before Jesus called Peter and his partners into discipleship—the smell of the fishy sea, the splashing of the oars, the swooshing of the nets, the creaking of the boat, and the swapping of fish stories. And it was like the old days in another respect: "that night they caught nothing."

Finally, the first rays of the morning sun cut paths through the dusky, foggy air, and when the fishermen looked toward the shore, they saw a man.

"Do you have any food?" he asked them.

"No," they chorused.

"Cast the net on the right side of the ship, and ye shall find," the man instructed. And the authority behind his words persuaded the disciples to give it a try.

It was a net-stretching, heavy-very-heavy-load-of-fish experience. Peter, Andrew, James, and John could remember a similar experience. That's what made them take a closer look at the man on the shore.

"It is the Lord," John exclaimed to Peter.

That did it. Peter wasn't going to waste any time in getting to the Lord. He grabbed his coat, jumped into the water, and swam to the shore (verse 7). The others brought in the ship and the netful of fish.

Jesus had everything prepared for a hearty, tangy breakfast. Fish were already frying over a fire of hot coals. And hot rolls were on hand.

If Peter didn't think about that fire, I'd be very surprised. It must have reminded him of another fire, the one in the palace courtyard. There he had stood warming himself while his heart grew colder and colder toward Christ. There he had denied Christ three times.

After breakfast, Jesus asked Peter, "Simon, son of Jonas, lovest thou me more than these?" (verse 15).

What did Jesus mean by this? I believe it was a question carefully tailored to help Peter look honestly at himself and see what he was really like.

First, consider the name Jesus used. It wasn't Peter, the "rock"; it was Simon. Jesus wanted to show Peter how his denial had proven that he was not yet a rock—solid, firm, dependable. Since Simon was the first name Jesus used in addressing Peter when they met for the first time (John 1:42), it seems Jesus was telling Peter that it was time to make a fresh start.

In asking Peter if he loved Him, Jesus used a word meaning the strongest kind of love—a selfless, sacrificing kind of love. In denying Jesus three times, Peter had shown self-love instead of love for Christ. He had acted in a cowardly manner in order to save his own skin. Unless he loved Christ enough to put His interests above his own, he could not be trusted with leadership in the church.

"More than these?" Why would Jesus ask Peter if he loved Him more than the other disciples loved Him? Again, I believe He was firmly but gently leading Peter into a healthy self-analysis. He wanted to cure him of self-reliance and get his faith centered on Him. The question must have chased Peter's mind down memory lane to the time he bragged that his devotion to Jesus Christ was stronger than that of the other disciples. "Though all men shall be offended because of thee, yet will I never be offended," he had boasted.

Peter had learned by bitter, hard experience that it just doesn't pay to put confidence in the flesh. His bragging days were over. Using a weaker word for love than Jesus used in asking if he loved Him more than the others did, Peter replied, "Yea, Lord; thou knowest that I love thee" (verse 15). Peter said in effect, "Lord, you know that I'm fond of you."

"Feed my lambs," Jesus said.

Then He asked Peter a second time, using the same strong word for love, "Simon, son of Jonas, lovest thou me?" And again, Peter employed the weaker word for love. "Yea, Lord; thou knowest that I love [am fond of] thee" (verse 16).

"Feed my sheep," Jesus said.

A third time, Jesus asked, "Simon, son of Jonas, lovest thou me?" This time, though, Jesus used Peter's word for love. He was asking in effect, "Peter, do you have even the kind of love for me that you profess to have? Are you truly fond of me?"

Having been asked three times if he loved

Jesus, Peter broke down. "Lord, thou knowest all things; thou knowest that I love thee," he offered (verse 17).

Jesus replied, "Feed my sheep."

The work of restoring Peter was over. Just as he had denied Christ three times beside an open fire, so now he had confessed to Jesus three times beside an open fire that he loved Him. Furthermore, none of that former brash self-reliance remained in him. He had been reluctant to say he loved Jesus with a selfless, self-sacrificing love. At last, emptied of vain pride, he was ready to assume a leadership role among the Lord's people. Now, knowing how dependent he was on Christ, Peter would stand firm as a "rock" against temptation and persecution.

The dialogue between the Lord and Peter holds important lessons on Christian service. We can recognize, as Peter did, that it is foolish to boast about our love for Jesus. It is best to be aware of the human tendency to fail our Lord unless we rely resolutely on Him. Furthermore, we need to realize that we serve Christ on behalf of His people. Believers are *His* lambs and sheep, not ours. We have no right to act as though those whom we lead are ours to order around and use for selfish purposes. Our responsibility is to feed Christ's sheep, not to fleece them.

Jesus continued His talk with Peter by predicting his manner of death. "When thou wast young, thou girdedst thyself, and walkedst whither thou wouldest," He told him, "but when thou shalt be old, thou shalt stretch forth thy hands, and another shall gird thee, and carry thee whither thou wouldest not" (verse 18). At one time Peter pledged that he would follow his Lord into the jaws of death, but he wasn't ready to do so until he had seen how weak he really was. Now, restored and cured of self-pride, Peter was open to the Lord's control and power, and ultimately he would die for the sake of Christ.

Many Bible teachers find in Jesus' words a prediction that Peter would be crucified upside down. And, if tradition is correct, that is precisely how he died. Tradition claims that in A.D. 69 or 70, Peter was in prison for his Christian witness and then taken from prison to face execution. When the executioners were going to nail him to a cross, Peter said, "No, no! My Lord died like that. I am not worthy to die as He did. Hang me on that cross head downward."

After predicting Peter's death, Jesus said, "Follow me."

Peter took Him literally. He started to walk along the shore behind Jesus. Then Peter glanced over his shoulder and saw John trailing along. "Lord, and what shall this man do?" Peter asked.

Haven't you heard that question in your church? So often, someone feels the Lord isn't treating him fairly. He feels that the Lord has given him more than his fair share of the work and would like to see others take on equal work assignments.

Jesus' reply to Peter is classic. Just what

each of us needs to hear when we feel the Lord is giving us more than our fair share of work or a tougher assignment than others have received. "If I will that he tarry till I come, what is that to thee? follow thou me" (verse 22). It is our Lord's prerogative to draw different plans for different Christians. It isn't up to me to question those plans or to demand that He show them to me. My responsibility is to accept His plan for my life and carry it out by His grace.

According to Jesus' prediction, Peter would not die until he was old, so he still had a lot of living to do. And that living would spill over to thousands for their spiritual good.

8
Dynamic Leadership

For forty days after the resurrection Jesus fellowshiped with His disciples and taught them truths pertaining to the kingdom of God (Acts 1:3). It must have been a rich spiritual experience for the disciples as they spent time with their risen Lord and learned the truths He taught. None of them knew, of course, just how soon they would have to impart those same truths to others.

On the fortieth day Jesus led His disciples from Jerusalem to Bethany, on the eastern slope of the Mount of Olives (Luke 24:50a). The inevitable farewell meeting had arrived. Jesus promised His disciples that they would be baptized with the Holy Spirit in a few days. This would be an historic event, for the Holy Spirit, the Comforter, would take up

His permanent abode in them. Thus, in-dwelled by the Holy Spirit, they would be objects of His ministry. He would encourage them, comfort them, keep them, guide them into all truth, develop godliness in them, and give them power for serving Christ effectively.

The disciples must have felt that they were standing on the threshold of the kingdom. After all, Jesus was alive—risen from the dead; He had been instructing them in kingdom truths; and now He had promised the arrival of the Holy Spirit in just a few days. All the conditions seemed to be right, so it is no wonder the disciples chorused, "Lord, wilt thou at this time restore again the kingdom to Israel?" (Acts 1:6).

What an answer Jesus gave! It must have rocked them back in their sandals. "It is not for you to know the times or the seasons, which the Father hath put in his own power" (verse 7).

I find Jesus' answer particularly apropos for our time, when so many are absorbed with prophecy. More than a few teachers of prophecy point out that conditions are ripe for Jesus' return for the church: Israel is in her own land; Russia is poised on the door-step of the Middle East; a ten-nation organization exists in Europe; and, because of computer technology, it is conceivable that every person in the world could be assigned an identification number. Some prophetic teachers are so sure of their ability to discern the times and the seasons that they resolutely claim Jesus will come for His church by the end of this decade. And, occasionally one emerges who is willing to predict the month, day, and year when the rapture will occur. In reply to all this date setting, I would insist that it is best to leave God's prophetic schedule in God's hands while we devote ourselves to the unfinished task of evangelizing the world.

In effect Jesus told His disciples to concern themselves with evangelism. He promised that the Holy Spirit would come upon them and give them power to be His witnesses "in Jerusalem, and in all Judea, and in Samaria, and unto the uttermost part of the earth" (verse 8). Fishing for men would have no limits!

As soon as He had spoken these words, Jesus lifted His hands and blessed the disciples (Luke 24:50b). Then, a cloud, likely the same cloud which had engulfed Jesus on the Mount of Transfiguration, the Shekinah glory cloud, received Him out of their sight (Acts 1:9). It was a fitting way for Jesus to leave His followers. He had commissioned them to do the greatest work on earth, and He had given them a scene to remember, that of His ascending to Heaven with His hands extended toward them as a gesture of blessing.

Have you ever said goodbye to a loved one at an airport, then watched as the airplane took off into the sky? Do you remember how you stood silently for awhile, looking pensively and melancholically at the point in the sky where the plane disappeared from your sight? If you have, then you can understand to some degree how the disciples must have felt when they stood on the Olivet hillside with their eyes focused on the sky after Jesus had ascended. It took the comforting words of two heavenly messengers to bring them out of the clouds. "Ye men of Galilee," they said, "why stand ye gazing up into heaven? this same Jesus, which is taken up from you into heaven, shall so come in like manner as ye have seen him go into heaven" (verse 11). Upon hearing this, the disciples walked back to Jerusalem, entered an upper room, and devoted themselves to prayer (verses 12-14).

Jesus had returned to Heaven, but He would come back to the earth again. This was the comforting message of the heavenly messengers. It was not as though Jesus had scrapped His plans for setting up His kingdom upon the earth. The disciples could rest assured that someday their risen Saviour would descend visibly and gloriously to the Mount of Olives and usher in earth's brightest day, the Kingdom Age. This would all come about just as the Old Testament prophet, Zechariah, predicted:

"And his feet shall stand in that day upon the mount of Olives, which is before Jerusalem on the east. . . . And the Lord shall be king over all the earth: in that day shall there be one Lord, and his name one" (Zechariah 14:4,9).

From this point in Peter's biography it becomes increasingly easy to see the finishing touches being applied by the divine Potter. We can see readily how Peter emerges as a useful and valuable vessel. For instance, on the Mount of Olives, the old Peter might have tried to talk Jesus into establishing the kingdom right away. And he might have brushed aside Jesus' instruction to wait at Jerusalem for the Spirit's power and insisted that he didn't need any help. But for the greatest part the old Peter had been stripped away and left on the shore where Jesus confronted him with the question, "Lovest thou me?" As we continue our study of Peter's life, we'll see him in a far more favorable light. We'll watch him fill the multiple roles of dynamic leader, wise spokesman, and powerful witness.

The disciples left the Mount of Olives and returned to Jerusalem, where they entered the upper room. There, along with others, they gave themselves to prayer. Acts 1:15 sets the number at 120. It was to this group that Peter addressed himself, suggesting on the basis of Psalm 69:25 and Psalm 109:8 that Judas' place as an apostle should be taken by another.

Personally, I am encouraged by the fact that Peter assumed this kind of leadership. He acted in accordance with the Lord's appointment of him as a leader in the church, and he based his remarks to the group on the Scriptures. He knew that his Lord had wiped the slate clean and given him a destiny to fulfill. There was nothing to be gained by living under a cloud of guilt, feeling worthless. Similarly, it doesn't serve any good purpose for a restored Christian to "cry over spilled milk" and sit on the sidelines watching others serve the Lord. The cause of Christ is best served in believing that the Lord forgives, forgets, and leaves us on the earth to serve Him enthusiastically, joyfully, and confidently.

I am also encouraged by the fact that the believers in the upper room accepted Peter's leadership. No hard feelings against Peter because he had denied the Lord! Showing a submissive attitude toward the Scriptures, they followed Peter's suggestion and narrowed the choice of a successor to Judas to two men, "Joseph called Barsabas, who was surnamed Justus, and Matthias" (Acts 1:23). Then they prayed, asking the Lord to show them which of the two should become the twelfth apostle (verse 24).

Following prayer, the disciples cast lots to determine the Lord's choice. Likely they put Matthias' name on one stone and Justus' name on the other, placed both stones in an urn, shook the urn vigorously, tipped it upside down, and let the stones tumble out. The first stone out carried the winner's name. In this case it was Matthias.

The tenth day of prayer in the upper room coincided with the Day of Pentecost, a holy day for the Jews. Meaning "fiftieth," Pentecost fell fifty days after the opening of the harvest by offering the first sheaves of grain to the Lord. It was a fitting time for God to reach down to Jerusalem and reap an abundant harvest of souls. Acts 2:1-4 sets the stage.

> "And when the day of Pentecost was fully come, they were all with one accord in one place. And suddenly there came a sound from heaven as of a rushing mighty wind, and it filled all the house where they were sitting. And there appeared unto them cloven tongues like as of fire, and it sat upon each of them. And they were all filled with the Holy Ghost, and began to speak with other tongues, as the Spirit gave them utterance."

What happened to the believers on that historic Day of Pentecost was indeed significant. The Holy Spirit came upon them and gave them the ability to proclaim God's wonderful works in languages they had never spoken before. Leaving the upper room, they spilled out into the street and made their way to the temple grounds. There they found a huge crowd of Jews from foreign countries. Parthians, Medes, Elamites, and others from Mesopotamia, Cappadocia, Pontus, Asia, Phrygia, Pamphylia, Egypt, Libya, and Rome. Cretans and Arabians were there too. All had come to Jerusalem to observe the Feast of Pentecost, but none of them had anticipated hearing about God in their native languages from a group of Galileans. No wonder they were astonished and asked one another, "What meaneth this?" (verse 12).

Although all the disciples spoke about God in foreign languages, Peter was the one who stepped forward with an explanation. Assuming the leadership Christ had appointed him to, he delivered his first sermon. And what a sermon it was! It honored Christ as Saviour and risen Lord in a clear, Scripturally based, and courageous manner. The contrast between this bold preaching and Peter's dismal denial of Christ in the palace courtyard is indeed convincing proof that grace can rescue us from our failures and make us strong servants of God.

Beginning by referring to the prophet Joel, Peter explained that the events of the day had been born of the Holy Spirit in fulfillment of Joel's prophecy. Then he riveted the crowd's attention on Jesus Christ, declaring that He was Saviour and risen Lord.

It has always been true that when the Holy Spirit controls a believer, as He did Peter, Jesus Christ is honored as the exalted Son of God. This in fact is one of the tests of Holy Spirit induced teaching and preaching. The Lord Jesus promised that the Comforter, whom He would send, would glorify Him (John 16:14a).

On pulpits facing some pastors when they stand to preach are the words, "Sir, we would see Jesus." This is appropriate, because people need to hear about Jesus Christ in all His saving grace and sovereign glory. On the Day of Pentecost, the assembled Jews received such a verbal portrait of Christ.

Faithfully, Peter declared that Jesus was the suffering servant of Jehovah. His credentials were fully authenticated by His "miracles, wonders, and signs" (Acts 2:22). Looking his audience straight in the eye, Peter accused them of having rejected and crucified this One whom God had approved as Israel's Messiah. "Him . . . ye have taken, and by wicked hands have crucified and slain," he charged (verse 23).

It is noteworthy that the crucifixion theme was central in Peter's sermon. Many times the Lord had struggled with Peter's slowness to accept the fact that He had come to earth to die on the cross for sinners, but now Peter was fully committed to that truth. The Holy Spirit had written indelibly upon Peter's heart the message that Christ had indeed come to offer Himself on the cross as our Saviour. It is interesting to observe that in Peter's first epistle the sufferings of Jesus Christ still maintained a prominent place in his teachings.

Continuing his sermon, Peter assured his Jewish listeners that Christ arose from the grave and was exalted to the right hand of God (verses 24,36). In this exalted position He holds the highest title, "Lord," and exercises the greatest power, that of saving all who call upon Him.

Heavy conviction of sin gripped those who heard Peter's message. Acts 2:37 says, "Now when they heard this, they were pricked in their heart, and said unto Peter and to the rest of the apostles, Men and brethren, what shall we do?''

Again, assuming apostolic leadership, Peter instructed his audience to repent—change their minds about Jesus Christ—and be baptized (verse 38). Their being baptized would declare the fact that God had forgiven their sins in response to their faith in His Son. Three thousand gladly heeded Peter's instructions. They turned to Christ in faith, were baptized, and became a closely knit fellowship of believers. Thus, the church at Jerusalem had its birth.

Under the discipling ministry of Peter and the other apostles, the church at Jerusalem became a model for all subsequent churches. Its members grew in grace, knowledge, love and service in exemplary fashion.

Wilberforce, a great English preacher, once commented that Christianity could be summed up in four words: *admit, submit, commit,* and *transmit.* The church at Jerusalem measured up to this concise description of Christianity, for the converts admitted their need of salvation through faith in Christ, submitted themselves to the apostles' teachings, committed themselves to the Lord and to one another, and transmitted the gospel to others (verses 42-46). As a result of hearing the good news of Christ and seeing His love and power in the believers' lives, an increasing number of men and women turned to Christ and became members of the church.

No question about it, the Lord had fully restored Peter from his sin of denying Him and had established him as a foundation stone in the church. This contrast in Peter's life was unmistakably clear at Pentecost, and it would become even more obvious in the months and years ahead.

9
Apostle With Authority

Peter and John were close companions. They were fishing partners when Jesus called them to leave their nets and boats and follow Him (Luke 5:10). They were sent by Jesus to prepare the Passover (Luke 22:8). Also, they ran together to Jesus' tomb on resurrection day (John 20:1-5). Now, as we read Acts 3:1, we learn that they went to the temple together for a 3 o'clock prayer service.

If it seems strange that these two apostles were still observing Jewish forms of worship, let us remember that God had not yet removed His offer of salvation from Israel. He was still graciously and persistently dealing with that nation, confronting it with the messianic claims of Jesus Christ. Eventually He withdrew His major attention from Israel and turned to the Gentiles, offering them the gospel. From that pivotal point until now His program for Israel has been suspended, and it will not resume until the church, comprised of born-again Jews and Gentiles, has been raptured. Furthermore, it would be some time before the apostles fully realized that Christ's death fulfilled the Jewish law, thereby ending the need for the law's observances. That realization would come mainly through the Apostle Paul's teaching (for example, Romans 10:4; Galatians 3:19-25; Ephesians 2:11-18; and Colossians 2:10-17).

Herod's Temple was a magnificent structure, with its impressive gates, colonnaded porches, courtyards, and sanctuary. After entering the temple area, Peter and John passed through the Court of the Gentiles and came to the Beautiful Gate which led into the Court of the Women, where the services of sacrifice and prayer were held. This ornate gate probably stood at the north end of Solomon's Porch which overlooked the valley of Kidron and the Garden of Gethsemane. Its doors were constructed of the finest Corinthian brass, and its exquisite workmanship made it worthy of the name "Beautiful."

But something was less than beautiful at the gate when Peter and John approached, for a crippled beggar lay there. According to Acts 3:2 and 4:22, he was over 40 years old and had been lame from birth. Daily, he had been carried to the temple by friends and placed by the Beautiful Gate so that he might beg money from worshipers. How typical of Israel he was! There, in the midst of religious activity, he was poor and helpless, just as Israel was spiritually impoverished and unable to walk in God's ways in spite of her religious surroundings and ceremonial observances. Today, too, in the midst of religion there is impoverishment and helplessness on the part of all who depend upon religion to do for them what only the power of Christ can accomplish.

When the lame beggar asked Peter and John for a donation, "Peter, fastening his eyes upon him with John, said, Look on us" (Acts 3:4).

With high hopes of receiving some money from Peter and John, the beggar riveted his attention on them (verse 5). "Then Peter said, Silver and gold have I none; but such as I have give I thee: In the name of Jesus Christ of Nazareth rise up and walk" (verse 6).

We can readily see in this episode the rock-like quality Jesus had developed in Peter. Although he was in the most revered place in the Jewish capital and surrounded by Jewish onlookers, Peter did not hesitate to speak in the name of Jesus Christ. Fully aware of the authority Christ had given His apostles, Peter commanded the lame beggar to get up and walk. Then, taking him by the right hand, Peter pulled him up; "and immediately his feet and ankle bones received strength. And he leaping up stood, and walked, and entered with them into the temple, walking, and leaping, and praising God" (verses 7,8). By the power of the risen Christ, Peter had given the lame man something far better than money; he had given him healthy feet and strong ankles. Indeed he had given him a new life. Yet, Peter was not the healer. He was simply the channel through whom the Great Physician, Jesus Christ, delivered divine healing.

In the book of Acts we read about a number of miracles performed by the apostles, and we may wonder why we don't perform such miracles. The answer is simple: the apostolic miracles were intended to serve a special purpose during a special time. Their purpose was to authenticate the apostles' message until they completed their Spirit-guided writing of the divinely inspired New Testament. Once the New Testament was in written form there was no further need of miracles. Today, in our witnessing and preaching, we can prove that our message is true by appealing to the New Testament.

The response to the miracle of healing was almost immediate. Everyone in the temple was flabbergasted at seeing the familiar temple beggar walking and praising God. At first, they stood in awestruck silence as they tried to figure out what had happened to him (verses 9,10). Then, upon seeing him hold Peter and John, they rushed to Solomon's porch for a closer look at the three men (verse 11). This sudden assembling of inquisitive worshipers gave Peter a great opportunity to preach about Christ. So, amid the colonnades, where the scribes often lectured and debated (Luke 2:46; 19:47; Mark 11:27), Peter gave a large number of Jews a clear presentation of the gospel.

Is there a preacher anywhere who wouldn't welcome the opportunity of preaching the gospel to a crowd? I don't think so. The big question is, how can a church attract a crowd? Some church members seem to feel that the pastor must attract the unsaved. They expect him to be a kind of pied piper of Hamelin, able to cast a spell over people and lead them into the church's auditorium. It doesn't matter to them what methods he uses for capturing a crowd. Swallowing goldfish while standing on a Sunday School bus, skydiving into the church's parking lot, letting the Sunday School class with the most visitors throw cream pies in his face, wrestling an alligator, or boxing a kangaroo—all are approved methods, if they draw a crowd. But isn't there a less ostentatious way to gain an audience for the preaching of the gospel, a way that involves the members of a church as well as their pastor? The answer is a resounding yes!

Why did the worshipers at the temple flock to Solomon's porch, thereby giving Peter a ready-made audience? They did so because three factors combined to create an impressive situation. 1) God did something extraordinary in the beggar's life. 2) The beggar publicly demonstrated what God had done in his life. 3) He joyfully gave God the credit for what had happened in his life. We dare not underestimate the results which could occur if these same factors were prevalent in twentieth-century Christianity. Surely, our churches would be crowded every Sunday if God's people were evidencing His wonderful work in their lives and telling others how good He is.

Peter wasted no time in directing his audience's attention from what had happened to who made it happen. He assured them that God had made the beggar strong through faith in Jesus Christ (Acts 3:12-16). This was God's way of glorifying "his Son Jesus," Peter testified (verse 13). He explained further that Jesus had been treated ruthlessly and despicably by the Jewish nation. He accused his audience of having delivered Jesus up for crucifixion, denying Him in the presence of Pilate and setting free a murderer instead of Him when Pilate gave them the opportunity to set a prisoner free. They had "killed the Prince of life, whom God hath raised from the dead," Peter charged (verse 15). But they had done this "through ignorance," Peter explained (verse 17).

Continuing his sermon, Peter declared how the sufferings of Jesus Christ on the cross fulfilled the predictions made by Israel's prophets (verse 18). Israel's responsibility now was to "repent . . . and be converted" (verse 19). This demanded a change of mind on the part of the Jews. They must recognize that they crucified the Messiah and turn in faith to Him for forgiveness. If they complied with this demand for repentance and a turning to Christ, God would reciprocate by 1) blotting out their sins (verse 9), 2) ushering in "the times of refreshing," and 3) sending Jesus Christ to them (verse 20).

The blotting out of Israel's sins was certainly not a new concept. In the Old Testament book of Isaiah, this blessing was anticipated:

"I, even I, am he that blotteth out thy transgressions for mine own sake, and will not remember thy sins" (43:25).

"I have blotted out, as a thick cloud, thy transgressions, and, as a cloud, thy sins: return unto me; for I have redeemed thee" (44:22).

Interestingly, the book of Isaiah is comprised of two divisions. The first division, chapters 1 through 39, carries the theme of divine judgment. Woes are pronounced upon Gentile nations and upon Judah and Israel in this division because of their sins. The second division, chapters 40-66, emphasizes God's willingness to forgive those who turn from their wicked ways and look to Jehovah for forgiveness (see 45:22 and 55:6,7). It is appropriate, therefore, that God's promise to blot out Israel's sins is found in the second division of Isaiah. Furthermore, it is interesting that the central chapter of that division, chapter 53, vividly depicts the redemptive work of Jesus Christ. God's forgiveness for Israel and us is based squarely on Jesus' offering of Himself on the cross as the sacrifice for our sins. Referring to Jesus' substitutionary death, Isaiah declared:

> "Surely he hath borne our griefs, and carried our sorrows: yet we did esteem him stricken, smitten of God, and afflicted. But he was wounded for our transgressions, he was bruised for our iniquities: the chastisement of our peace was upon him; and with his stripes we are healed. All we like sheep have gone astray; we have turned every one to his own way; and the Lord hath laid on him the iniquity of us all" (Isaiah 53:4-6).

In calling upon Israel to repent and be converted, Peter was pointing the nation to the crucified Saviour, whose death on the cross provided the way for God to blot out sin.

In ancient times, the ink used for writing on papyrus sheets did not contain acid, so it did not bite into the papyrus. It was relatively easy, therefore, to use a wet sponge and erase what had been written. In pardoning a condemned man, for example, an official would wipe away from the papyrus sheet all the written charges. We can readily see how appropriate it is to speak of God's blotting out transgressions, for His forgiveness involves a complete removal of our sins and all the charges that were against us.

If Israel had responded favorably to Peter's plea for repentance and faith in Jesus Christ, the conditions would have been ripe for Jesus' return to establish the messianic kingdom in fulfillment of the many Old Testament prophecies about Israel's golden age. However, as we know from the book of Acts, Israel rejected every opportunity to turn to the Lord Jesus Christ, including this one in the temple area.

Still preaching with a sense of the authority Jesus Christ had committed to him, Peter warned his audience about the grave consequences of rejecting Christ, whom he identified as a prophet like Moses (verse 22). He foretold, "And it shall come to pass, that every soul, which will not hear that prophet, shall be destroyed from among the people" (verse 23). The choice was clear: Repent and be converted, and God's blessings will come in superabundance; or reject Christ, and be destroyed—shut out forever from God and His blessings.

Isn't there a similar choice today? A person may trust in Christ as Saviour and thereby become the recipient of God's copious blessings: forgiveness, life, peace, assurance, joy, to name a few; or he may reject Christ and thereby seal his destiny— separation from God in a state of eternal punishment. John 3:36 summarizes the difference this way:

"He that believeth on the Son hath everlasting life: and he that believeth not the Son shall not see life; but the wrath of God abideth on him."

Peter faithfully delivered to Israel the message of the crucified and risen Saviour, and he confronted his audience with a choice. According to Acts 4:4, "many of them which heard the word believed." May we, too, faithfully deliver the message of Christ to others and give them a clear choice. So many need the opportunity, and surely the results will be worth all our efforts to reach them for Christ.

10
Big Trouble.
Bigger Faith.

At Caesarea Philippi Jesus predicted that the gates of hell would storm His church but not prevail against it. Prior to the fourth chapter of Acts we don't read about any attacks on the church, but we can be sure the enemies of Christ and His church were anything but happy with the way things were going. The message about Jesus' death and resurrection was taking hold in Jerusalem. Thousands had already believed on Him. You can be sure that the Jewish authorities were ready to explode in rage against the church, and especially against Peter and John. Acts, chapter 4, registers the first shock waves of that explosion.

Word spread quickly from the temple that Peter and John were speaking to a large throng of worshipers. Very soon, this news reached the Jewish authorities, so that while Peter and John were still speaking to their audience, "the priests, and the captain of the temple, and the Sadducees, came upon them" (Acts 4:1). Verse 2 indicates that these officials were particularly distressed because the apostles were preaching the resurrection of Jesus Christ and its promise of resurrection for all who trust in Him. The Sadducees, as the theological liberals of Judaism, despised the concept of a resurrection. There simply was no room in their theology for such supernatural intervention by God into the normal course of human life and death. The priests of Judaism were divided into twenty-four courses, with each course on duty for a week at the temple. Likely the priests referred to in verse 1 were on duty when Peter and John were preaching. Since many of the priests were Sadducees, we can understand why they, too, were infuriated that the apostles taught the resurrection. The captain of the temple was second in command in the temple hierarchy. Having command of the temple guards, he was outranked only by the high priest. So it was an impressive assortment of officials who converged on Peter and John to drag them away for trial, just as priests and temple guards had converged on Jesus in the Garden of Gethsemane and carried Him off for trial. Peter and John were about to experience a fulfillment of Jesus' predictions about the persecution which would befall His disciples:

> "Remember the word that I said unto you, the servant is not greater than his lord. If they have persecuted me, they will also persecute you" (John 15:20a).

> "Behold, I send you forth as sheep in the midst of wolves: be ye therefore wise as serpents, and harmless as doves. But beware of men: for they will deliver you up to the councils, and they will scourge you in their synagogues" (Matthew 10:16,17).

> "But take heed to yourselves: for they shall deliver you up to councils; and in the synagogues ye shall be beaten: and ye shall be brought before rulers and kings for my sake, for a testimony against them" (Mark 13:9).

Acts 4:3 discloses that the Jewish authorities put Peter and John into prison, likely one of the rooms in the temple. Since it was already evening, it would be difficult to convene a meeting of the Sanhedrin, so the apostles' trial would have to wait until the next morning.

Since the healing of the lame man took place near 3 p.m. and it was evening when Peter and John were arrested, obviously the impromptu preaching service lasted at least three hours. So, for at least three hours, people listened to a sermon. But the length of the sermon didn't perturb the listeners, for its message was refreshing. It was about resurrection. It focused on the power of God's risen Son to transform lives, even as He had transformed the apostles from despondent disciples hiding behind closed doors "for fear of the Jews" (John 20:19) into aggressive ambassadors of Christ. It pulsated with hope, forgiveness, and the promise of eternal life. Nothing the crowd had heard before compared with this message, so three hours of listening to Peter and John must have seemed very brief.

Peter and John were thrown into jail, but the Word of God cannot be bound. It penetrated the hearts of those who heard Peter and John preach it, and it created faith in many. Acts 4:4 tells us that enough men believed the message to raise the number of male believers in Jerusalem to 5000.

The following morning, Peter and John were brought before the Sanhedrin, the supreme Jewish court (verses 5-7). Annas the high priest and Caiaphas, his son-in-law, were on hand for this trial, undoubtedly hoping to deal a fatal blow to the infant church. After all, these two had been the ringleaders in plotting the crucifixion of the Lord Jesus Christ. They certainly didn't want any talk of Jesus' resurrection to continue.

It took tremendous courage for Peter and John to remain loyal to Christ in the presence of these enemies of the cross. But all the stamina they needed was supplied by the Holy Spirit.

"By what power, or by what name, have ye

done this?" the Sanhedrin inquired, obviously referring to the healing of the temple beggar.

Rising to the occasion and assuming his role of leading spokesman among the apostles, Peter seized the question as a golden opportunity to preach Christ to the Sanhedrin. What a contrast this was to the time he stood fearfully in the high priest's courtyard and denied His Lord three times! Now, standing eyeball to eyeball with the high priest, he spoke boldly about his Lord. He made it plain that he and John were being tried unjustly, for they had done a good deed in healing the temple beggar (verse 9). The real criminals, according to Peter, were the Sanhedrin members, for they were guilty of rejecting and crucifying Jesus Christ, whom God later raised from the dead (verses 10,11). Furthermore, Peter declared, salvation is available only through Jesus Christ (verse 12).

The Sanhedrin was stunned and stumped. They marvelled at the boldness with which Peter and John had conducted themselves. Although they had never attended a rabbinic school, Peter and John had not backed down an inch in front of the distinguished Sanhedrin. Their conduct and words convinced the Sanhedrin that "they had been with Jesus" (verse 13). Furthermore, the healed temple beggar was standing alongside Peter and John as Exhibit A in their defense (verse 14). How could the members of the council deny that a miracle had been performed, and how could they condemn Peter and John for what they had done? They couldn't. So, after a brief strategy huddle, they ordered Peter and John "not to speak at all nor teach in the name of Jesus" (verse 18).

Again, the boldness of Peter and John was evident. They replied: "Whether it be right in the sight of God to hearken unto you more than unto God, judge ye. For we cannot but speak the things which we have seen and heard" (verses 19,20).

Further threats came from the Sanhedrin, but finally it released Peter and John, fearing an adverse reaction from the people who had witnessed the miracle and were glorifying God for what He had done (verse 21).

It didn't take the two apostles any time at all to decide their course of action. They went to their fellow believers and gave them a full report of what had transpired (verse 23). This prompted a praise and prayer meeting in which the believers exulted in God's sovereign will and power and asked Him to give them boldness to keep on declaring the Word and performing miracles in Jesus' name (verses 24-30).

Great things resulted from this praise and prayer meeting. The place where it was held shook, and the believers were all filled with the Holy Spirit. They spoke the Word of God boldly (verse 31). They were knit together in unity, and out of love for one another shared their goods, so that no one lacked food, clothing, or shelter (verses 32-37). It was a warm climate of love and goodwill that was just right for the apostles' preaching Christ with power (verse 33), because whenever believers evidence unity and love, preaching is more readily believed.

Peter had met persecution head-on and by faith in Christ and love for Him had weathered the storm. He and John had gone before the Sanhedrin determined to be faithful to the Lord. And, just as the Lord had stood by Daniel in the lions' den centuries before, so He stood by Peter and John in the den of vicious lions which was called the Sanhedrin. Like Daniel, Peter and John had emerged unharmed, while the lions paced back and forth feeling cheated that they hadn't been able to land a single bite.

Persecution takes rather mild forms in the Free World—ridicule, exclusion from certain social circles, and sometimes the withholding of job promotions, to name a few—but even these mild forms of persecution provide Christians with an opportunity to stand firm in the faith. Like Peter, we can follow the route of doing good, sharing the good news of Christ with others, choosing to obey God in the face of threats, and keeping company with fellow Christians who provide a loving fellowship of prayer, kindness, and evangelistic outreach.

Peter had assumed praiseworthy leadership in the way he had met the trouble that came from the enemies of Christ, and soon he would have to assume similar leadership in dealing with trouble that emerged from within the church.

Acts 5 carries the account of the first serious problem that raised its head in the church. Perhaps Ananias and his wife, Sapphira, had been jealous of Barnabas because, according to Acts 4:36,37, he had sold land and given the money to the apostles. They must have felt there was a lot of glory to be gained by their doing the same thing, so they sold some property. Then, Ananias went alone to the apostles and presented what was supposed to be the full sale money. In reality, though, he and Sapphira had kept back part of the money for themselves (Acts 5:1,2).

Realizing that Ananias was only feigning dedication to the Lord, Peter confronted him with his sin. "Ananias," he asked, "why hath Satan filled thine heart to lie to the Holy Ghost, and to keep back part of the price of the land?" (verse 3). He explained that Ananias was under no obligation to give any of the money to the Lord, but in pretending to give all of it to the Lord he had lied to God (verse 4).

Instantly, Ananias fell down dead. Young men wrapped him in burial cloth, carried him out, and buried him (verse 6). God's judgment had been swift.

About three hours later, Sapphira appeared before the congregation. Perhaps she had been on a shopping spree or had been at home planning one when her husband took their offering to church. At any rate, she didn't know what had happened to her husband. So she was in for a shock.

Peter asked her whether she had sold the land for the amount of money her husband had presented as the total amount. When she replied, "Yes," Peter asked why she and her husband had conspired to put the Spirit of the Lord to a test. Then, he informed her about her husband's death and announced that she, too, would meet a similar fate (verses 8,9).

Instantly, she fell down at Peter's feet, died, and was carried away for burial next to her husband (verse 10).

God's judgment had come upon her, too.

Peter's handling of this sin in the church may seem harsh, but we ought to remember two things: 1) God hates hypocrisy, and 2) the church in its infancy needed a clear understanding of God's high standard of purity.

We would make a terrible mistake to think that our church leaders today should pronounce a death sentence upon all hypocrites in the church. The fact is, no one today has apostolic authority for acting as Peter acted. Nevertheless, our churches should be concerned about sin in their ranks and make every effort to exercise loving discipline. If we gloss over sin, allowing it to taint the testimony of our churches, we will pay a bitter price. The world will get a distorted view of our God and see little or no reason to believe the message we preach.

Sometimes a church is afraid to discipline sinning members, feeling that such discipline will drive people away from the church. This reasoning, of course, is un-biblical. Acts 5:11-14 tells us that the dis-ciplining of Ananias and Sapphira profound-ly affected the church for the best. The church members gained a deeper respect for God's holiness, and many outside the church became believers and joined the church.

Before long, the whole city of Jerusalem was feeling the impact of the ministry of Peter and the other apostles. Many were healed of infirmities, and many trusted in Christ. But this didn't spell an end to the trouble Peter faced. Soon the high priest and Sadducees arrested Peter and the others, and threw them into the common prison (verses 17,18).

The jail term didn't last long though, because the angel of the Lord opened the prison doors during the night and escorted the apostles to freedom. In doing so, He commanded them to "Go, stand and speak in the temple to the people all the words of this life" (verse 20).

Just as soon as the first rays of the sun beamed over Jerusalem, the fearless apostles were back at the temple, teaching the people. The high priest and the rest of the Sanhedrin found this out only after sending guards to the apostles' empty cells and hear-ing from a messenger that the apostles were at the temple (verses 21-25). Quickly, the Sanhedrin's guards rushed to the temple, ap-prehended the apostles, and brought them before the council (verse 26).

The high priest was appalled to think that

the apostles had disobeyed the Sanhedrin's earlier command that they stop teaching and speaking in Jesus' name. "Behold, ye have filled Jerusalem with your doctrine, and intend to bring this man's blood upon us," he charged.

Again, assuming his leadership role, Peter boldly declared the apostles' loyalty to God. Then he boldly accused the Jewish authorities of crucifying Jesus, whom God raised from the dead to be a Prince and a Saviour, through whom forgiveness was available to Israel (verses 29-32).

The Sanhedrin fell under heavy conviction, but its members were unwilling to repent. The conviction soon turned to white-hot anger as they discussed how they might kill the apostles (verse 33).

One of their number, Gamaliel, a Pharisee of great reputation among the Jews, convinced the rest not to kill the apostles but rather leave their fate in God's hands (verses 34-39). The council accepted Gamaliel's advice, beat the apostles, ordered them once more not to speak in the name of Jesus, and released them (verse 40).

The persecution Peter faced this time was greater than it had been in the past, but it did not deter him and the other apostles from serving Jesus Christ. Verse 41 discloses that he and his co-workers left the council "rejoicing that they were counted worthy to suffer shame for his name." And verse 42 indicates that they kept on teaching and preaching Christ every day in the temple and in every house.

Peter and the other apostles were a minority in Jerusalem, but they were a resolute minority. Nothing could deter them from taking a stand for Jesus Christ. Persecution made them stronger, just as storms make trees stronger by their sending roots down deeper into the soil. Through faith in the Lord, they were invincible. May it be true of us, as we face persecution in whatever form it takes, that we resolutely trust in the Lord and take our stand for Him.

There's a story about a woman in the Colonies during the Revolutionary War. Upon hearing that the Redcoats were converging on her town, she snatched up a rolling pin from her kitchen and, holding it high, marched into the street.

"Where are you going?" her neighbors asked.

"I'm going to meet the British troops," she replied.

"Well, you're not going to be able to put up much of a fight with just a rolling pin," they advised.

"That may be so," she responded, "but at least they'll know which side I'm on."

Today, the world desperately needs to know which side we Christians are on. Let's take our stand for Christ and refuse to let any opposition snuff out our witness for Him.

11
Smoothing Another
Rough Spot on the Rock

The Jerusalem church grew vigorously, but it had its share of problems. The Ananias and Sapphira incident was the first of these. Soon, it was followed by a complaint from the Greek Jews in the church that their widows were not getting the kind of consideration the Hebrew widows were receiving in the daily distribution of food and other necessities. Acts 6 records this problem and shows how wisely it was resolved. The congregation elected seven godly men, all of them Greek Jews, to take charge of the daily distribution. Not long afterwards, though, one of those men, Stephen, was martyred—stoned to death—by the Sanhedrin. Then there emerged a bitter foe, Saul of Tarsus, a young Pharisee whose main goal in life was to destroy the church. His fury was so intense that believers scattered throughout Judea and Samaria to escape from him.

But trouble has always been a friend of the church as well as its foe, because it forces believers to depend more heavily upon the Lord and to take stock of their values. When Saul's persecution ravaged the Jerusalem church, the believers who fled to other parts of Judea and to Samaria, took the gospel with them (Acts 8:4). This resulted in churches being established throughout Judea and in Samaria. In reality, it took this persecution to push the believers from the big church in Jerusalem into some other places where Jesus wanted the gospel preached. Remember His commission in Acts 1:8? "Ye shall be witnesses unto me both in Jerusalem, and in all Judea, and in Samaria, and unto the uttermost part of the earth."

The story of how the Lord got the gospel beyond Judea and Samaria and into the Gentile world is the story of Saul of Tarsus' being converted to Christ and ordained by Him to be an Apostle to the Gentiles. But the story also includes Peter.

Acts 10 drops us into the seacoast community of Joppa, where we find Peter resting at the home of a tanner named Simon. He had just completed a preaching tour of Samaria and coastal towns, so a good vacation at the seaside was in order. But Peter's vacation was about to come to an end, because God had a new assignment for him.

If Joppa sounds familiar, it is likely so because you recall the story of Jonah. Centuries before Peter's lifetime, God commanded Jonah to go to Nineveh, a Gentile megalopolis, and denounce its wickedness. Because Jonah harbored prejudice against Gentiles and feared that God would forgive the Ninevites if they repented, he spurned God's command. Instead of going to Nineveh, he booked passage on a ship heading as far from Nineveh as it was possible to travel. One whale later, though, Jonah's attitude was different. When God repeated His command that he go to Nineveh and preach against it, Jonah obeyed promptly.

Peter's experience in Joppa was quite similar to Jonah's. God had to work on Peter's attitude before he was ready to accept an assignment to preach to a group of Gentiles in Caesarea, 25 miles up the coast from Joppa.

Cornelius, a Roman military officer in command of 100 soldiers, lived in Caesarea. Since he had an intense desire to please God, he led his family and servants in the worship of Jehovah, gave great sums of money to the needy, and prayed earnestly and regularly. One day, he received a vision in which an angel commended him for his devotion to God and instructed him to send men to Joppa. There they were to make contact with Peter at the home of Simon. Peter would instruct Cornelius in the will of God (verses 1-6).

Heeding the angel's words, Cornelius dispatched two of his servants and one of his soldiers to Joppa (verses 7,8).

While Cornelius' three messengers were on the road to Joppa, Peter was on the flat roof of Simon's home, and he was praying. Verse 9 reveals that he started this prayer vigil about "the sixth hour," 12 noon. We can only wonder if this time of day seemed especially significant to Peter, since it marked the mid-point of Jesus' sufferings on the cross on that infamous day of the crucifixion. Surely Peter's prayers must have included a deep expression of thanksgiving for his Saviour's great love in dying for his sins.

Peter was beginning to feel hungry. After all, it was noon, and the aroma of fresh seafood cooking downstairs was no respecter of prayer. His taste buds were urging him to pronounce a benediction and hurry downstairs to the kitchen, but "he fell into a trance" (verse 10). While in this trance, he saw a huge sheet, tied at its four corners, being lowered to him. He also saw that it contained a smorgasbord of "all manner of four-footed beasts of the earth, and wild beasts, and creeping things, and fowls of the air" (verse 12). Lots of potential food for a hungry man, but it wasn't *kosher*; it was all disallowed by the Mosaic law (see Leviticus 11). So, when a voice from heaven commanded, "Rise, Peter; kill, and eat" (verse 13), Peter refused on the grounds that he had "never eaten any thing that is common or unclean" (verse 14).

"What God hath cleansed, that call not thou common," the voice countered (verse 15).

The third time Peter protested the command to kill and eat, the sheet was taken up into heaven, leaving him bewildered about what it all meant.

Peter had changed a lot since being restored to fellowship with the Lord after the denial. The book of Acts depicts him as a Spirit-filled man, whose chief goal was to serve Christ faithfully. He did the right things, and he said the right things. How, then, do we account for this exception in Acts 10, this refusal to kill and eat what the Lord had prepared? The answer, I think, lies in the fact that human nature is as unpredictable as a so-called tamed tiger. Just as soon as we think everything is under control, an old instinct flares up. Even the most dedicated Christian is not immune; until he is forever with the Lord, he can experience occasional flareups of sinful self-assertion, feeling that he knows better than the Lord what should or should not be done. This is how it was with Peter. In refusing the Lord's offer of lunch, he had reverted to a habit of the past—correcting the Lord. No wonder the Bible cautions, "Let him that thinketh he standeth take heed lest he fall" (I Corinthians 10:12).

While he was puzzling over the meaning of the sheetfull of detestable edibles, the messengers from Cornelius arrived and asked for him (verses 17,18). The Spirit told

Peter that they were there and that he should go with them without any hesitation because the Spirit had sent them (verses 19,20).

Although Peter didn't understand right away what the lowered sheet signified, he did understand soon afterwards. We know this because, after accompanying the messengers the next day to the home of Cornelius, he said to Cornelius, Cornelius' assembled relatives, and his friends, "Ye know how that is an unlawful thing for a man that is a Jew to keep company, or come unto one of another nation; but God hath shewed me that I should not call any man common or unclean" (verse 28). He had learned that racial barriers are supposed to break down under the love of Christ.

By His death on the cross, Jesus Christ provided the way for Jews and Gentiles alike to have peace with God and be at peace with one another. In Christ, saved Jews and saved Gentiles are on an equal footing. Ephesians 2:11-16 explains this spiritual phenomenon.

Prejudice is an evil force. It insults the Creator, who made all men in His own image. It also insults the Saviour, who placed such a high value on all human life that He died for the sins of the whole world. Furthermore, it causes divisions in the family of God and opposes evangelism and missions. We dare not claim to have a burden for souls if we are only concerned about reaching souls wrapped in the same skin color as ours and having a cultural background similar to ours.

The early church struggled with prejudice

as an increasing number of Gentiles trusted in Christ. For a long time, Jews and Gentiles didn't mix well in the churches. It took a meeting of representatives of the churches in session with the apostles at Jerusalem to resolve the problem (Acts 15). That meeting, along with the Galatian and Ephesian letter, made it clear that saved Gentiles did not have to become Jews in order to be first-class citizens of Heaven.

In his mission to Cornelius, Peter discovered that God didn't make any distinctions between Jews and Gentiles. The way of salvation was the same for both groups. Later, at the Jerusalem council session, Peter stood firm on this point. He told the representatives of the churches:

> "Men and brethren, ye know how that a good while ago God made choice among us, that the Gentiles by my mouth should hear the word of the gospel, and believe. And God . . . put no difference between us and them, purifying their hearts by faith. . . . But we believe that through the grace of the Lord Jesus Christ we shall be saved, even as they" (Acts 15:7-11).

Unfortunately, there is one recorded instance when Peter acted later as though he believed that saved Gentiles were not as good as saved Jews. It happened in a dining room at Antioch. Until Jews from Jerusalem showed up, Peter was enjoying a hearty meal with a group of Gentile Christians. But, when the Jews arrived, he left his Gentile luncheoners and moved to the Jews' table. This brought a sharp rebuke from the Apostle Paul (Galatians 2:11-14), as well it should have, because even one act of prejudice is out of character for a man of God.

At Cornelius' home, everything was just right for a preaching service. Not only did Cornelius want to be saved, he wanted his relatives and friends to be saved too, so he packed them into his house. Then, too, Peter was on hand because he believed God had arranged the meeting. And, he had the right message for the congregation.

Peter preached Christ, declaring that He had been anointed with the Holy Spirit and power, had ministered benevolently, and had been blessed by God. He explained that Jesus Christ was crucified but rose from the dead and was seen by His apostles. Further, Peter declared that the risen Christ had commanded His followers to preach about Him. Ordained of God to be mankind's Judge, Christ offers remission of sins to "whosoever believeth in him" (Acts 15:34-43).

Before he could finish his sermon, Peter and other Jews who had accompanied him to Caesarea witnessed an amazing event. The Holy Spirit fell on the listeners, signifying that they had believed on Christ and were saved (verses 44,45). These new-born believers spoke in tongues and magnified God (verse 46), just as the Jewish disciples had done at Pentecost. There was no doubt about it, these Gentiles had become forgiven sinners. So Peter commanded them to receive believers' baptism (verses 47,48).

After a brief stay in Caesarea, Peter went to Jerusalem, where he recounted to perturbed Jews the story of how God had brought salvation to Cornelius' household (Acts 11:1-17). Recognizing the truthfulness of Peter's report, these Jews "glorified God, saying, Then hath God also to the Gentiles granted repentance unto life" (verse 18).

At Caesarea-Philippi, Jesus had promised Peter the keys of the kingdom of heaven (Matthew 16:19). Later, at Pentecost, Peter used those keys to open the door of salvation for the Jews. At Cornelius' home he used those keys again to open the door of salvation for the Gentiles. On both occasions, he did this by preaching the gospel. Today and every day we can share the gospel with others and thereby give them an opportunity to enter into eternal life. Let's not let the keys get rusty.

12
Too Young To Die

Back in Jerusalem, Peter found a pack of trouble on the church's doorstep. Some very vocal Jews in the church were growling because Gentiles were professing faith in Christ without becoming Jews. But there were other growls. Stomachs were growling because a famine had struck Judea (Acts 11:27,28). If it hadn't been for the generosity of the Christians at Antioch, the hunger pains would have been unbearable (verses 29,30). Furthermore, Herod the king was growling; and it was his growl that brought Peter into an extremely perilous situation.

Acts 12:1 refers to Herod Agrippa I, the grandson of Herod the Great who ruled over Palestine when Jesus was born. Herod the Great, you may recall, tried to kill the infant

Jesus. Herod Agrippa I had inherited his grandfather's disposition. He was shrewd, self-seeking, vain, and vicious. In A.D. 37 he received from the Roman emperor, Gaius, the title of king, with territories northeast of Palestine as his kingdom. Two years later, Galilee and Perea were added to his kingdom. Then in A.D. 41, a new emperor, Claudius, tacked on Judea and Samaria to Herod's kingdom.

From Herod Agrippa's standpoint, the future must have looked promising. Surely, if he did a good job of ruling Judea and Samaria, his political fame and fortune would skyrocket. But Judea was a challenge, for its people despised the Romans. If he could only win the favor of the people, he'd have them eating out of his hand. In turn, the country would be calm, the emperor would be impressed, and he would be acclaimed as Herod the hero.

It didn't take Herod long to win the people's favor. He achieved his goal by singling out some of the church's leaders as targets of his wrath (Acts 12:1). When he beheaded James, the brother of John, and saw how delighted the Jews were over that action, he apprehended Peter and tossed him into a dungeon (verses 2-4). Since it was Passover Week and Jewish law forbade executions during Passover, Herod decided to postpone Peter's execution until after Passover. In the meantime, four squads of four soldiers each guarded Peter in shifts. Two soldiers were chained to him while the other two guarded the celldoor (verse 6). Herod and the guards must have thought that escape was impossible. But they failed to take two important facts into consideration. Peter belonged to the God of the impossible, and "prayer was made without ceasing of the church unto God for him" (verse 5).

The night preceding Peter's scheduled execution was anything but a nerve-jangling, sleepless night for the apostle. He slept soundly (verse 6). Even being chained to his guards didn't keep him from a sound sleep. Surely Peter knew he belonged to the God of the impossible and the church was praying for him. Also, Jesus had predicted that Peter would die as a martyr when he was old (John 21:18). Perhaps Peter reasoned, "Jesus made that prediction only fourteen years ago. I'm not old yet, so I'm not going to die for quite awhile. Since Jesus has always been true to His word, I may as well make the best of this bad situation by getting a good night's sleep." What a contrast to his former blustery ways this picture of Peter provides. He had truly learned to cast his care upon the Lord—something he later advised all believers to do (I Peter 5:7).

You may be in an extremely trying situation now, just as Peter was in an extremely trying situation in his dungeon cell. You may be facing a financial crisis. Or, perhaps your marriage is in jeopardy. Or, possibly you are finding it almost unbearable to deal with a serious health problem. Your son or daughter may be rebelling against your parental authority. Or, maybe conditions at work are intolerable. Whatever your difficult situation is, don't lose hope. Cast your care on the Lord, knowing that the same factors which worked in Peter's favor are working in your behalf as well: 1) You belong to the God of the impossible. 2) Fellow Christians are praying for you. (You have asked them to pray for you, haven't you?) 3) You have the Lord's reliable Word to count on. His promises about meeting your needs and seeing you through will not fail!

No doubt about it, Peter was in a very deep sleep in the prison. Even the brilliant light accompanying the arrival of the angel of the Lord didn't disturb his sleep. The angel had to punch him in the ribs and start pulling him to his feet to wake him up. "Arise up quickly," the angel told Peter; and, as he spoke these words, Peter's chains fell off (Acts 12:7).

Still giving directions, the angel told Peter to get dressed, tie his sandals onto his feet, throw on his cloak, and follow him (verse 8). Peter obeyed, but felt that he was seeing a vision. Then he followed the angel past two guard stations and through an iron gate that opened for them as though it were controlled by an electronic eye. Finally, they were standing in the street. That's where the angel left Peter and Peter became fully conscious that the Lord had delivered him (verses 9,10).

It may seem strange to us that James was beheaded while Peter was delivered. One sterling servant of God died, but the other lived. The reason lies locked up in the sovereignty of God. He fulfills His purposes in mysterious ways sometimes. But we can understand that His way is always best. James gained an early arrival in Heaven where He would see Christ and serve Him there; whereas Peter gained additional years of service for Christ on earth. We may never be able to understand why some Christians experience what seems to be an untimely death while others live to a ripe old age, nevertheless we can be sure that our heavenly Father doesn't make mistakes. Paul's approach to living and dying should help us to realize that we are winners regardless of how briefly or long we live on the earth. In Philippians 1:21,23,24 he wrote:

"For to me to live is Christ, and to die is gain. For I am in a strait betwixt two, having a desire to depart, and to be with Christ; which is far better: Nevertheless to abide in the flesh is more needful for you."

Soon, Peter went to the home of Mary, John Mark's mother. Many believers clustered inside, praying (Acts 12:12). We do not know for sure they were praying for Peter's deliverance from prison. They may have been praying that he would remain faithful to Christ even in martyrdom. After all, he had denied Christ once in his lifetime. At any rate, they should not have been surprised to find him at the door. But they were!

A young girl, named Rhoda, answered Peter's knocking at the door. She was so overjoyed and excited at finding Peter at the door that she forgot to let him in. She rushed back inside and told everyone that Peter was standing outside (verses 13,14). To put it bluntly, everyone thought she was crazy. She must have seen Peter's guardian angel, they thought (verse 15). But they couldn't deny that someone was out there, knocking and knocking. So, finally they answered the knocking and to their astonishment saw Peter at the door (verse 16).

Prayer meetings can be productive, often more productive than we expect. This was certainly true of the prayer meeting in the home of John Mark and his mother. God is only limited by our lack of faith.

I heard once about a past president of a seminary in the Southwestern United States who exhibited resolute faith in a critical situation. And his faith was promptly rewarded. The seminary was in debt and needed several thousand dollars right away. So several men, including the seminary president, huddled together for prayer. After a few of the men had prayed, the president prayed, "Lord, you own the cattle on a thousand hills. Please sell some of the cattle and send us the money." Before the prayer meeting ended, a cattleman arrived at the seminary and wrote a check to the seminary for an amount that covered the immediate need. In doing so, he stated that he had just sold some cattle and felt led to share the profit with the seminary.

Once inside, Peter told the group "how the Lord had brought him out of the prison." Further, he instructed them to relate this to James, the Lord's half-brother, and to the other believers (verse 17). Then he left for another place.

When morning arrived and Peter's escape was known, Herod ordered the execution of the guards who had custody of Peter (verse 19). Later, at Caesarea, this vain and vicious ruler was struck dead by the hand of God because he permitted his subjects to declare that he was a god (verses 19b-23). The cause of death was humiliating and grotesque, for "he was eaten of worms" (verse 23). God had dealt a fatal blow to the man who had tried to deal a fatal blow to the church. With the demise of Herod, "the word of God grew and multiplied" (verse 24).

The story of Peter begins to fade after he was delivered from prison. His subsequent ministry included participation in the Jerusalem Council (Acts 15), a trip to Antioch (Galatians 2:11-14), a visit to Corinth (I Corinthians 1:12; 9:5), and likely a tour of the eastern part of the empire where he ministered to Jewish Christians of the Diaspora (scattered Jews). His final residence was Babylon, from which he wrote his epistles, I and II Peter (see I Peter 5:13).

Bible scholars disagree over the meaning of Babylon in I Peter 5:13. Some believe the name applies to Rome, while others feel it applies to the ancient city of Babylon in the East. Regardless of this disagreement, all are persuaded that Peter suffered martyrdom by crucifixion at the hands of Nero. Generally, the date of his death is set at A.D. 67, and tradition states that he died at the age of 75.

In our brief survey of Peter's life, we have seen him in contrasting cameos—sometimes blustery, too quick to act and too slow to think, and at other times so devoted to Jesus Christ and so full of faith. We have seen the transforming power of Christ in Peter's life, as the Lord patiently and persistently shaped him into a rock. And, perhaps most importantly, we have seen so much of ourselves in Peter, and this has encouraged us to believe that the Lord can also mold us into strong, dependable believers. Let us, then, respond eagerly to Peter's last Scriptural exhortation.

"But grow in grace, and in the knowledge of our Lord and Saviour Jesus Christ. To him be glory both now and for ever. Amen" (II Peter 3:18).